Kingsville Ontario Book 2 and Area in Colour Photos, Saving Our History One Photo at a Time

Photography
by Barbara Raué
2015

Series Name:
Cruising Ontario

Book 124: Kingsville Book 2
and Area

Cover photo: 7005 County Road 46, Iron Kettle Bed and
Breakfast, Comber

Series Name: Cruising Ontario
Saving Our History One Photo at a Time
in colour photos

Books Available in Alphabetical Order:
Aberfoyle, Acton, Alton, Ancaster, Arthur, Aylmer, Ayr,
Bloomingdale, Brantford, Burlington, Caledon, Caledonia,
Cambridge, Clifford, Conestogo, Delhi, Dorchester to Aylmer,
Drayton, Drumbo, Dundas, Eden Mills, Elmira, Elora, Fergus,
Guelph, Hagersville, Hamilton, Hanover, Harriston, Hespeler,
Jarvis, Kitchener, Linwood, Listowel, London, Lucknow,
Mono, Mount Forest, Neustadt, New Hamburg, Niagara-on-
the-Lake, Oakville, Orangeville, Orillia, Owen Sound,
Palmerston, Peterborough, Port Elgin, Preston, Rockwood,
Seaforth, Sheffield, Shelburne, Simcoe, Southampton, St.
Jacobs, St. Thomas, Stoney Creek, Stratford, Tillsonburg,
Waterdown, Waterrford, Waterloo, Wellesley, Wingham

Other Books by Barbara Raue

Coins of Gold

Arrows, Indians and Love

The Life and Times of Barbara
Volume 1: Inventions That Have Enhanced My Life
Volume 2: Entertainment That I Have Enjoyed
Volume 3: East Coast Trips
Volume 4: Olympics Have Always Intrigued Me
Volume 5: Wonders of the World
Volume 6: Caribbean Cruises We Have Enjoyed
Volume 7: Animals
Volume 8: Storms and Other Major Disasters in My Lifetime
Volume 9: Wars, Terrorist Attacks and Major Disasters

The Cromwell Family Book

Laura Secord Discovered

Daddy Where Are You?

Visit Barbara's website to view all of her books
http://barbararaue.ca

Table of Contents

Kingsville

Kingsville is located in Essex County in southwestern Ontario, west of Leamington, south of Lakeshore, southeast of Essex. It is primarily an agricultural community nestled along the north shore of Lake Erie. The terrain is generally flat, and consists of a mixture of various rocks, sand and clay. The town is about 570 feet above sea level.

Kingsville is home to the Jack Miner Bird Sanctuary. Jack Miner was awarded The Order of the British Empire (OBE) for his achievements in conservation in the British Empire. Jack Miner is considered "the father of the conservation movement on the continent".

The Town of Kingsville is rich in history and Victorian era architecture.

Leamington

Leamington is located in Essex County, Ontario. It includes Point Pelee, the southernmost point of mainland Canada. Leamington became the home of the H. J. Heinz factory in 1908. The Heinz products were shipped from Leamington mostly to the United States. Ketchup and baby food were the main products. Leamington is known as the "Tomato Capital of Canada". The Heinz Company closed its plant in Leamington in 2014.

Leamington was incorporated as a village in 1876. The community was named after Royal Leamington Spa in England. It was a crossroads hamlet with about 300 residents and was first known for its lumber products. There were several docks, and fish were plentiful in Lake Erie and sturgeon could be speared from the shore; fish was the cheapest food available. Leamington once had many tobacco farms but now they are gone.

Blytheswood

Blytheswood is a small community located in Essex County, in southwestern Ontario. The village is at the intersection of Highway 77 and Concession 8. Blytheswood's more recognized businesses are the Jones Popcorn family farm and Setterington's farm supply depot. Blytheswood and the surrounding area of Leamington are experiencing a boom in greenhouse development for agricultural products.

Highway 77

King's Highway 77, commonly referred to as Highway 77, is a provincially maintained highway in the Canadian province of Ontario. One of three highways within Essex County, Highway 77 serves to interconnect Highway 3 near Leamington with Highway 401 near Tilbury.

Due to the flat topography of Essex County, the land use surrounding Highway 77 is almost entirely agricultural. Soil conditions in Essex are ideal for farming. Many streams have been diverted to irrigate the farmland to either side of the highway.

Highway 77 begins at the *Leamington Bypass*, north of the city of the same name. The western section of Highway 3 shares its eastern terminus with Highway 77; from there it travels west towards Windsor. Several greenhouses are visible near the southern end of the highway, a small percentage of the 610 hectares (1,500 acres) of land occupied by them in the Leamington area.

The highway runs seven miles north through Mount Carmel and Blytheswood to the village of Staples before turning to the east. It continues in this direction for a mile before returning to its northward orientation. North of there, the highway passes to the east of the Comber and District Historical Society Museum. The museum, which focuses on the history of agriculture, was established in the former Maple Grove Schoolhouse, which was built in 1894. Pressing north to Highway 401, Highway 77 passes Middle Road in the centre of Comber. Highway 401 provides access to Windsor and the United States to the west, and to the town of Tilbury and city of Chatham-Kent to the east. To the north, the road continues as Essex County Road 35 to Stoney Point on the shores of Lake Huron.

Tilbury

Tilbury is located in the municipality of Chatham-Kent and is 26.5 kilometres southwest of Chatham and 57 kilometres east of Windsor on Highway 401.

The nearby townships of Tilbury West in Essex County and Tilbury East in Kent County were named for the port of Tilbury in the English county of Essex. A settlement, called Henderson after the local postmaster, was established with the construction of the Canada Southern Railway in 1875. The name of the post office was changed to Tilbury Centre and later to Tilbury. Tilbury is famous for its murals which depict part of its history.

In 1998, the town was amalgamated with the City of Chatham and all municipalities of Kent County to form the municipality of Chatham-Kent. The former town hall at 17 Superior Street is now Tilbury Municipal Centre and Chatham-Kent Police station. Tilbury is home to a number of industries related mainly to the auto sector.

Kingsville

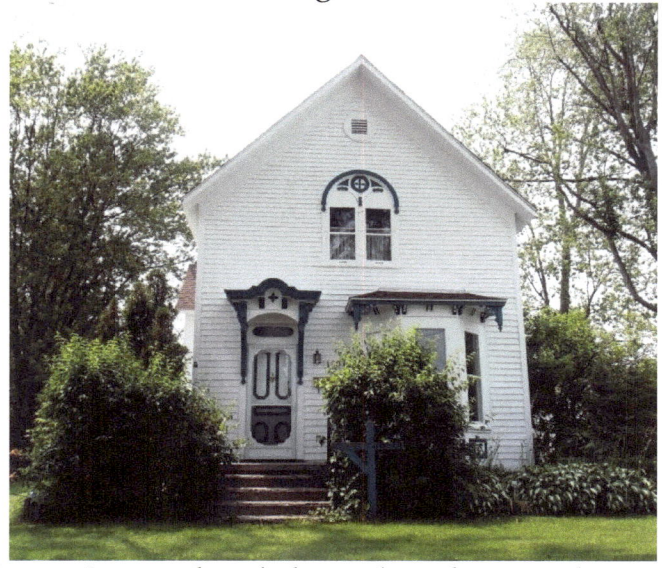

160 Queen Street – hood above door, bay window, cornice brackets

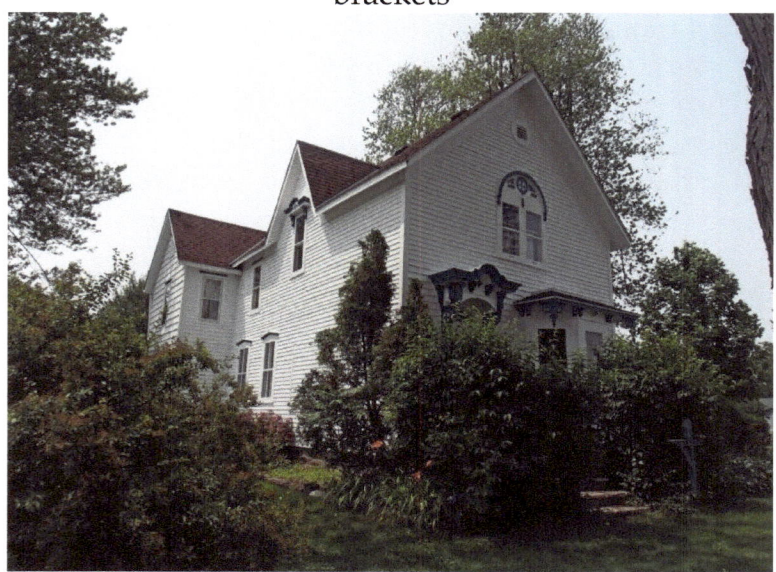

Window hood in side gable

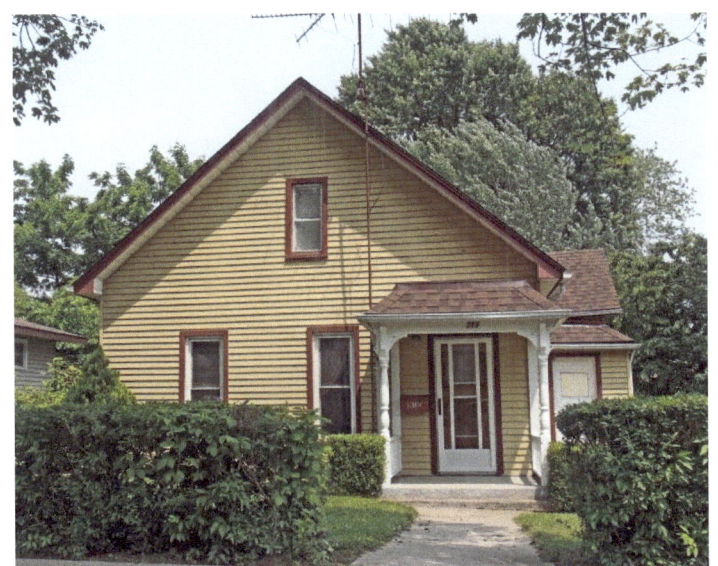

217 Queen Street - vernacular

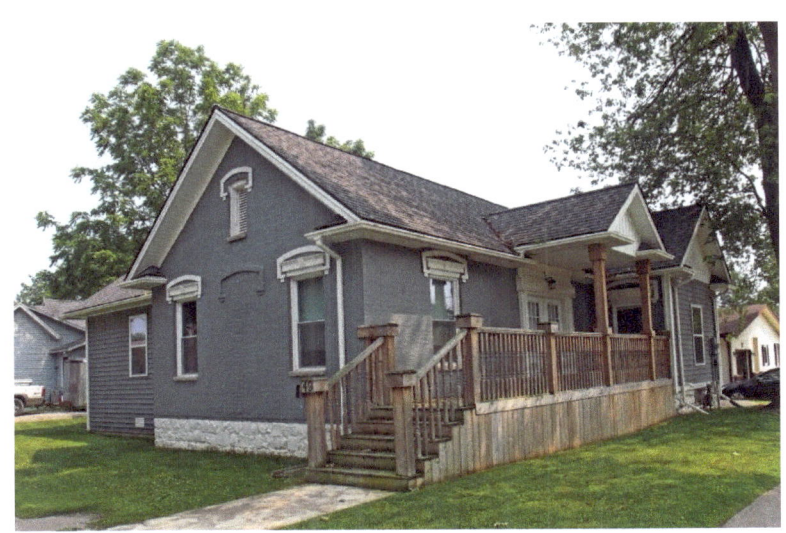

149 Queen Street

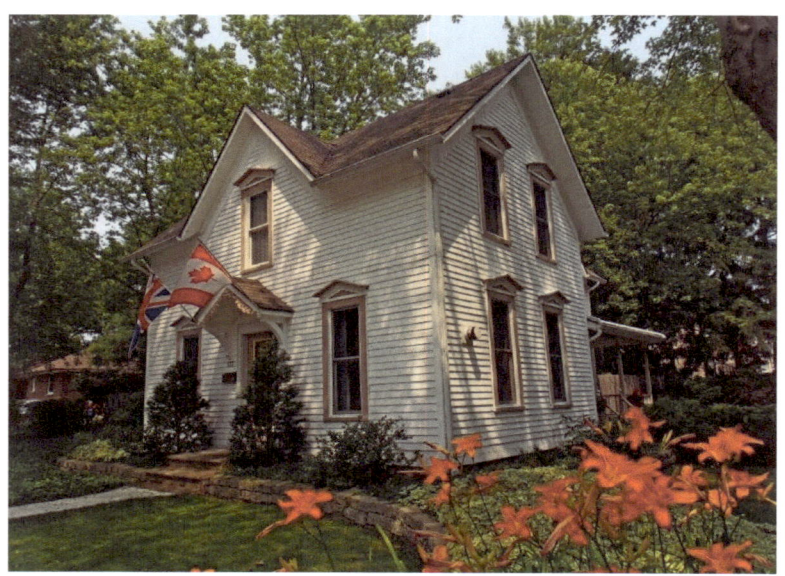

127 Queen Street – Gothic Revival – window hoods

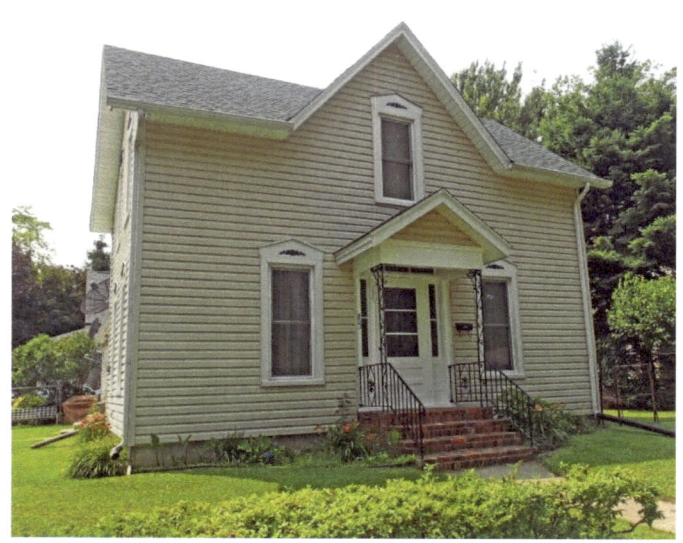

128 Queen Street – Gothic Revival

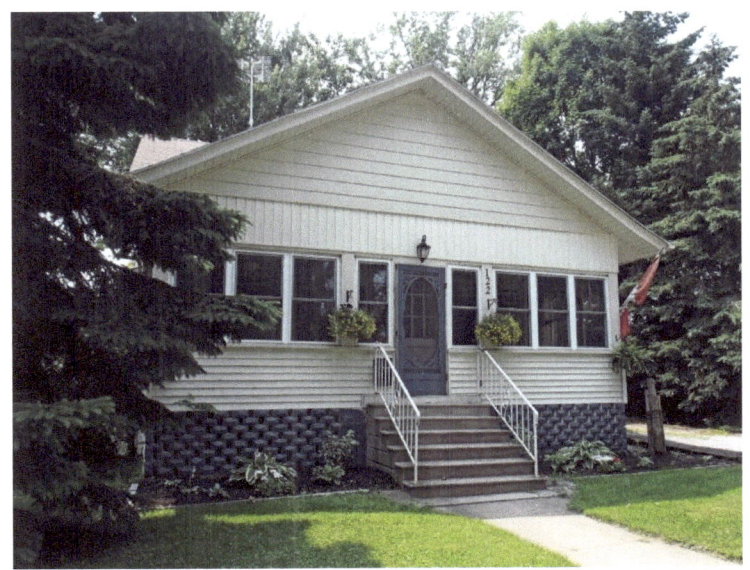

122 Queen Street - vernacular

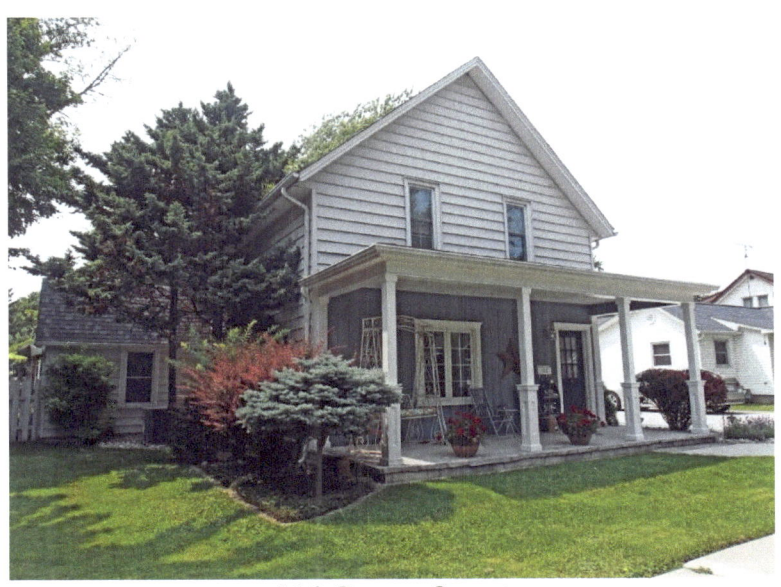

116 Queen Street

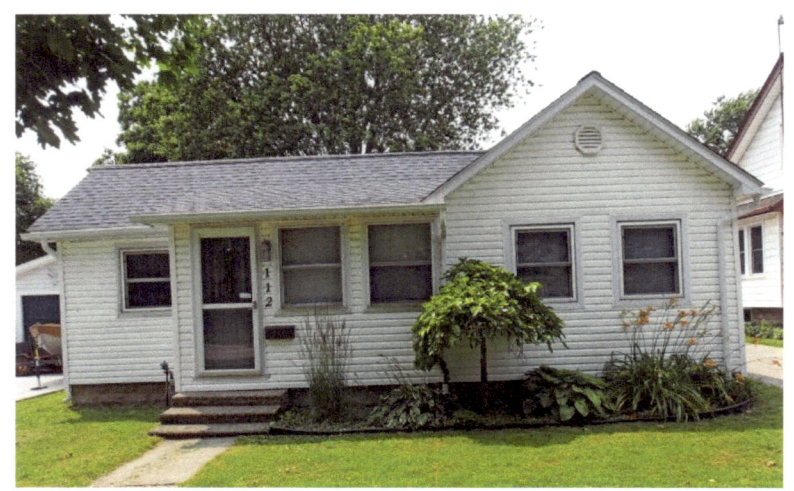

112 Queen Street

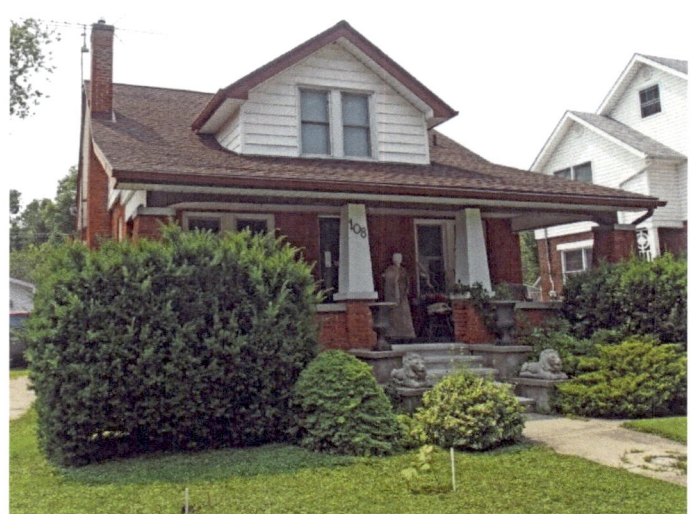

108 Queen Street - dormer

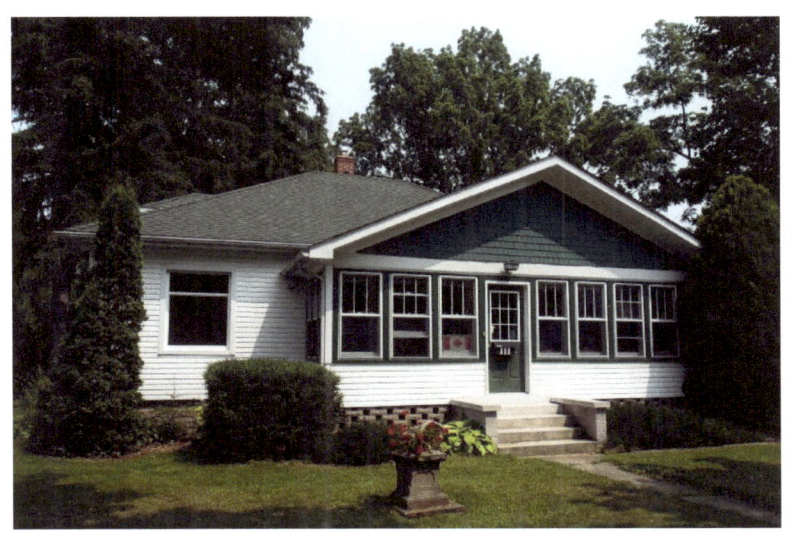

111 Queen Street - vernacular

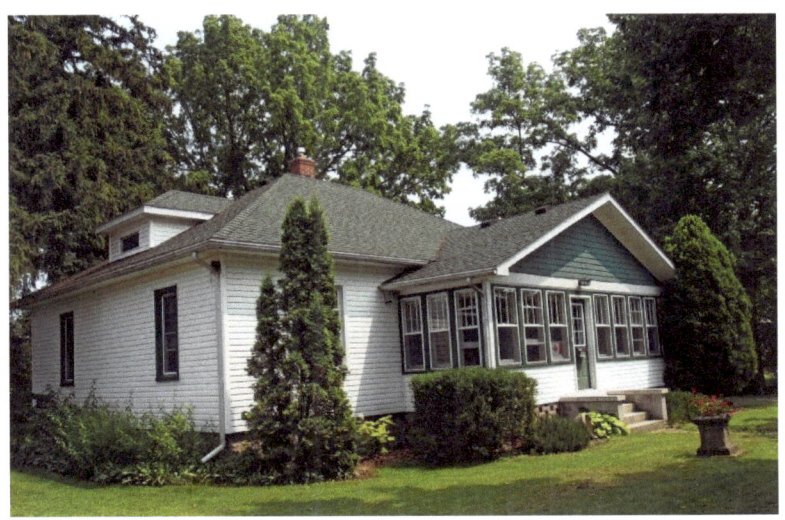

dormer

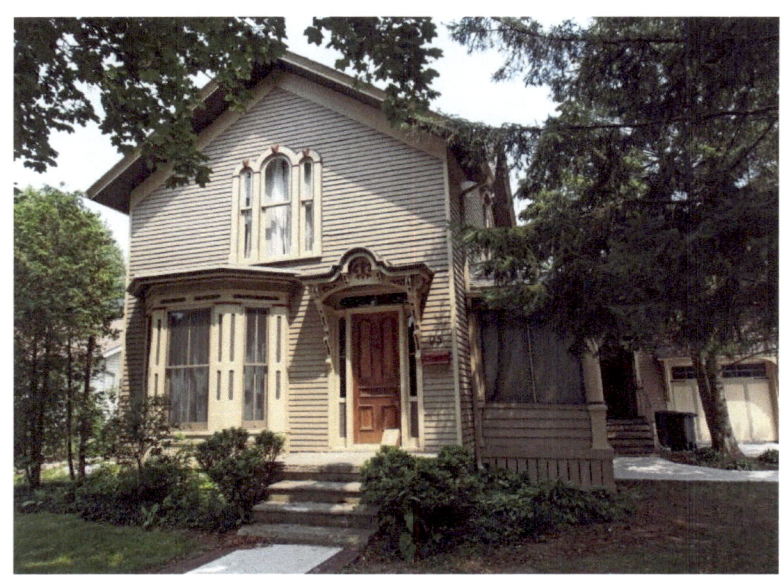

95 Queen Street – Palladian windows, bay window, hood above door

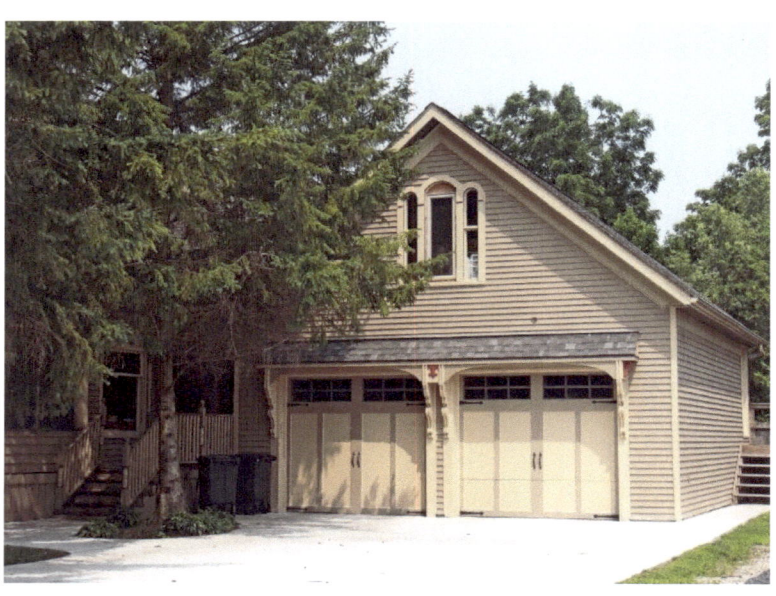

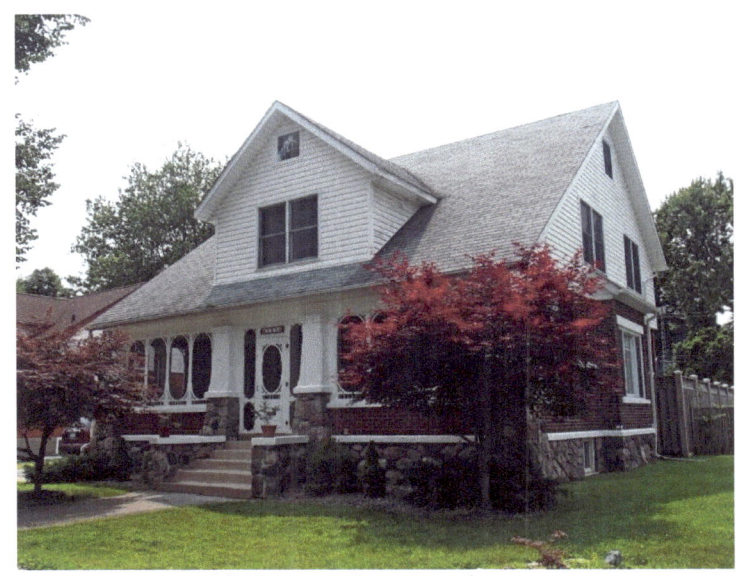

102 Queen Street - dormer

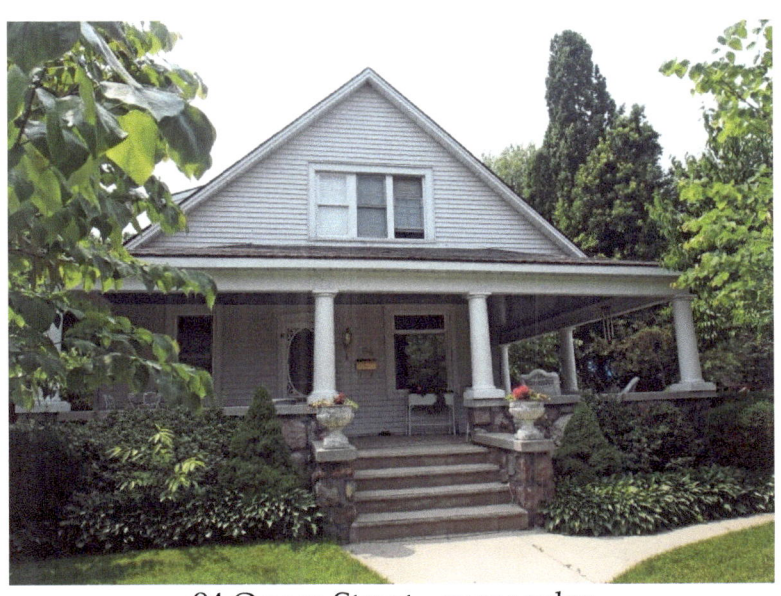

94 Queen Street - vernacular

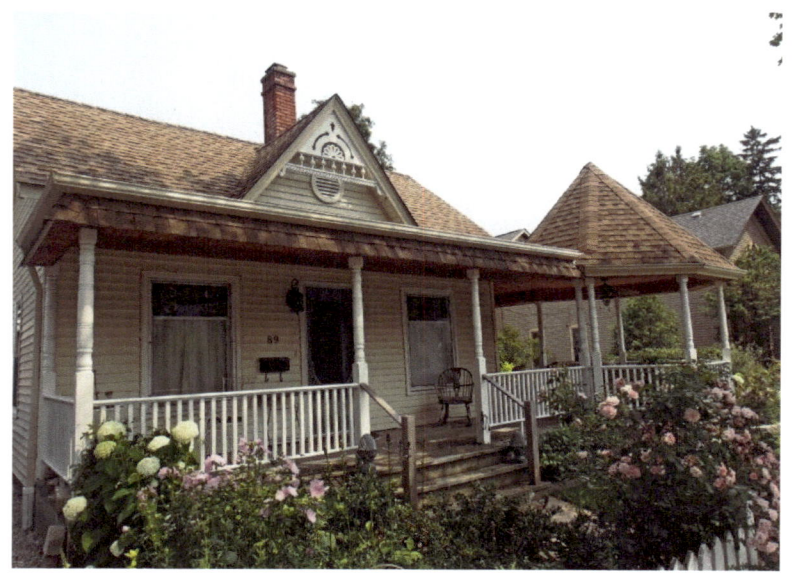

89 Queen Street – turned wooden spindles on verandah supports, spindles and stenciling on gable

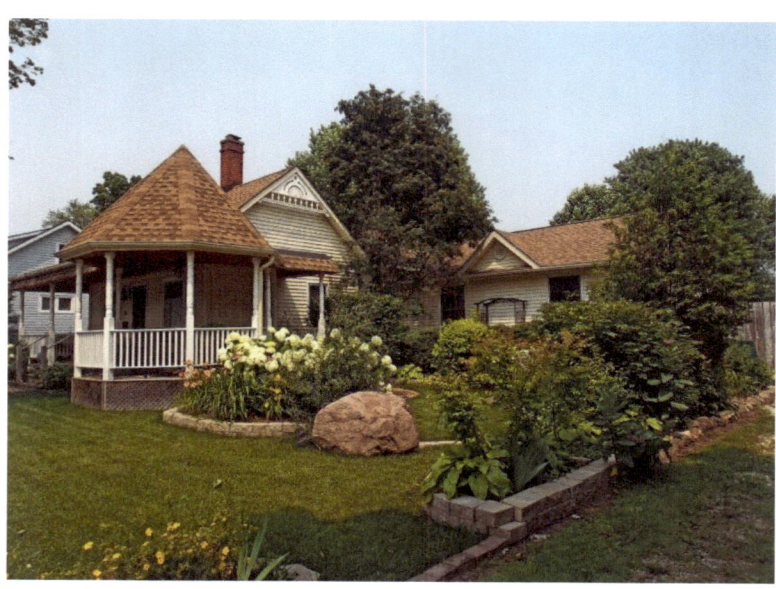

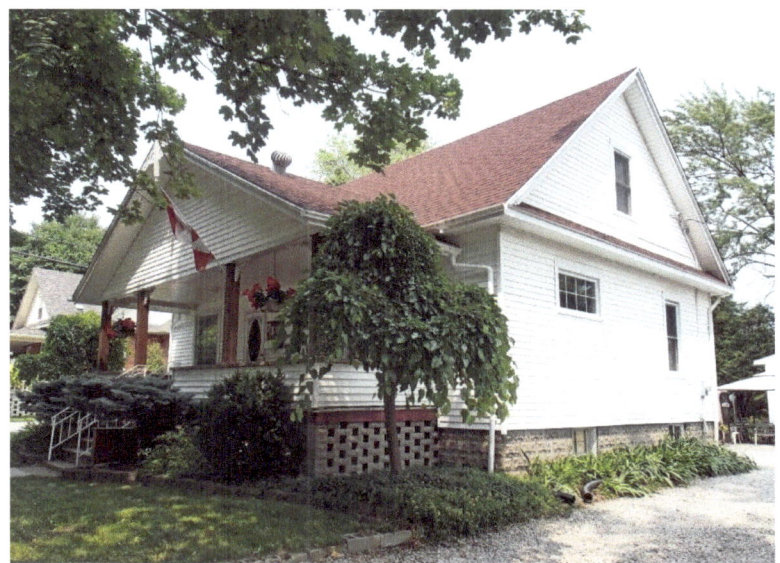

73 Queen Street – verge board and finial on front gable

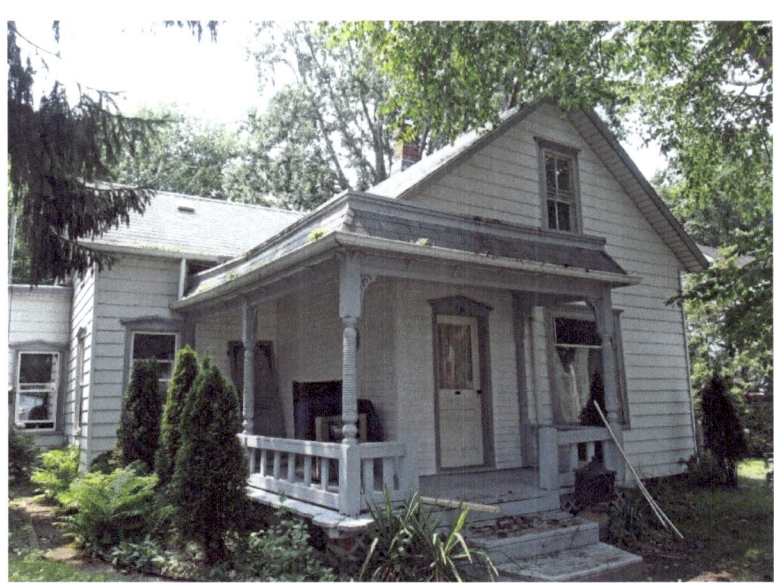

76 Queen Street – turned wooden spindles on porch supports

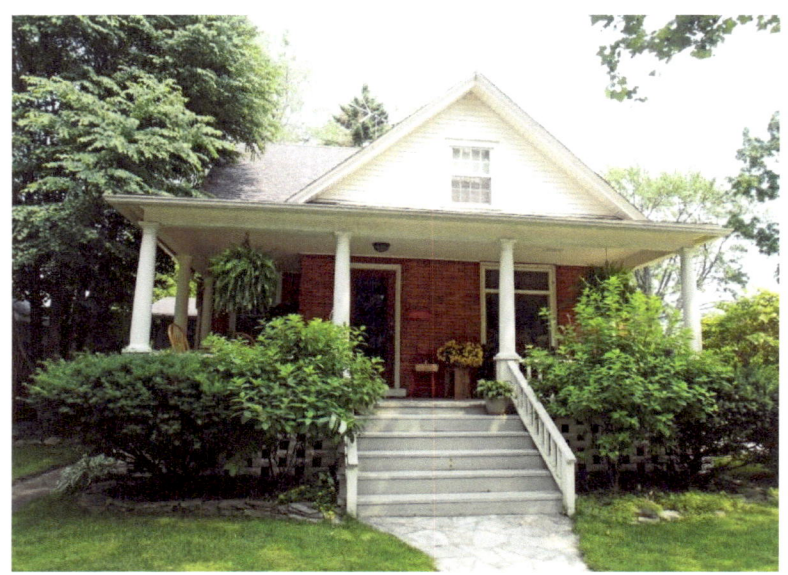

67 Queen Street - vernacular

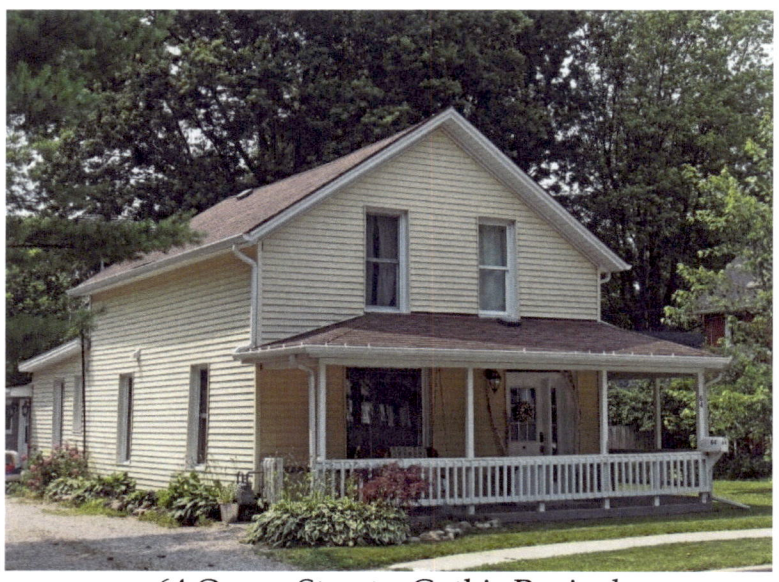

64 Queen Street – Gothic Revival

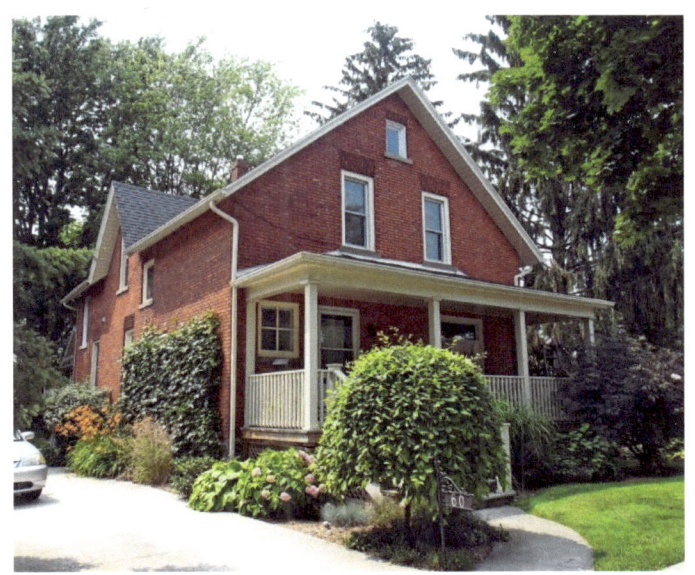

60 Queen Street – Gothic Revival

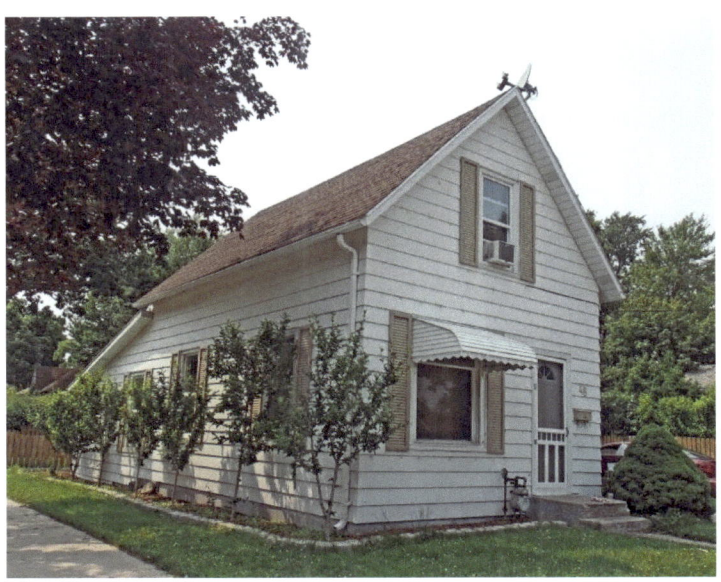

48 Queen Street – saltbox style

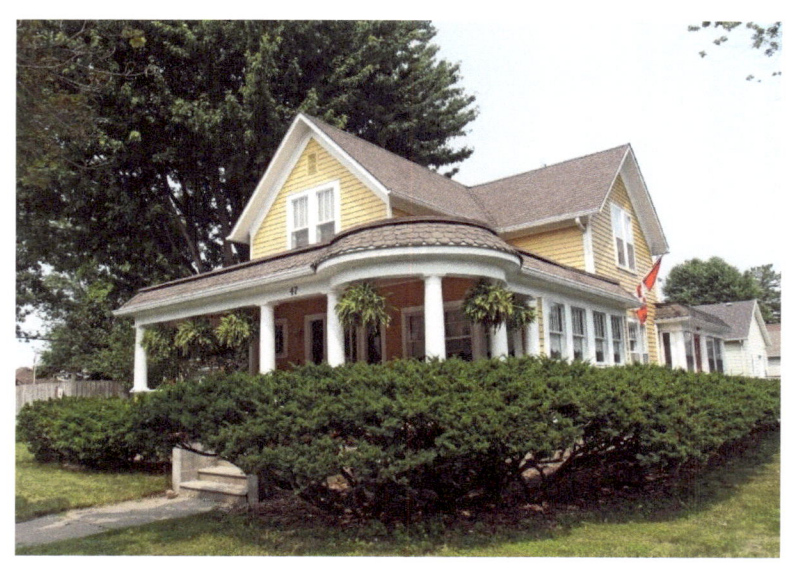

47 Queen Street

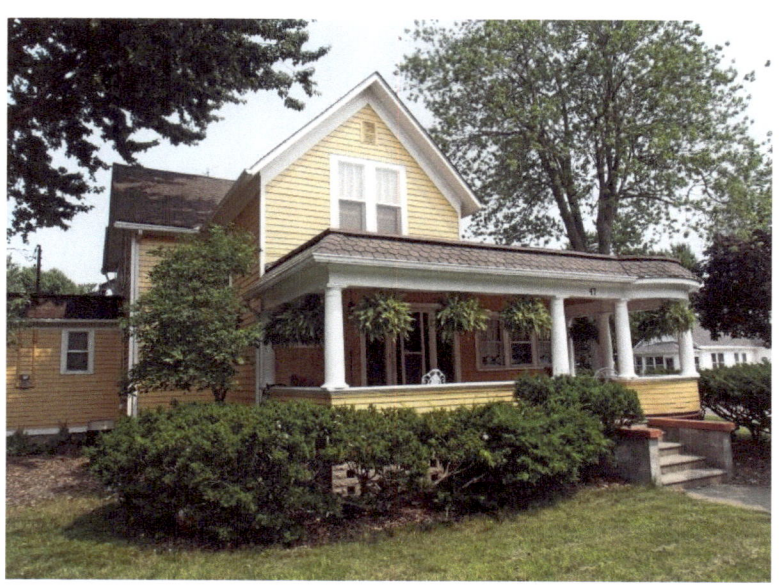

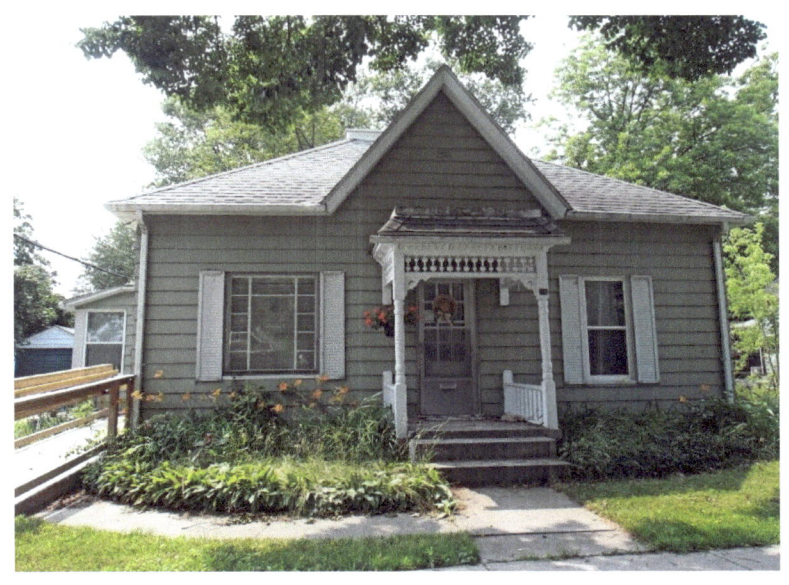

38 Queen Street – decorative entranceway with spindles

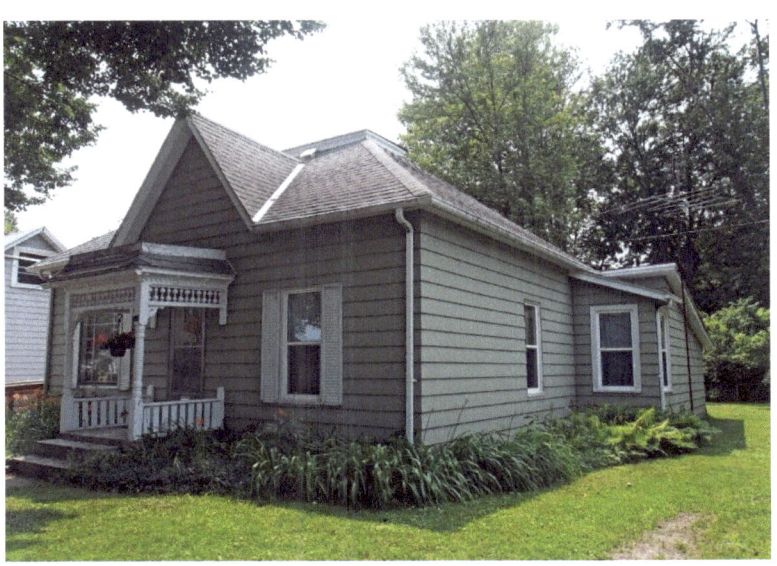

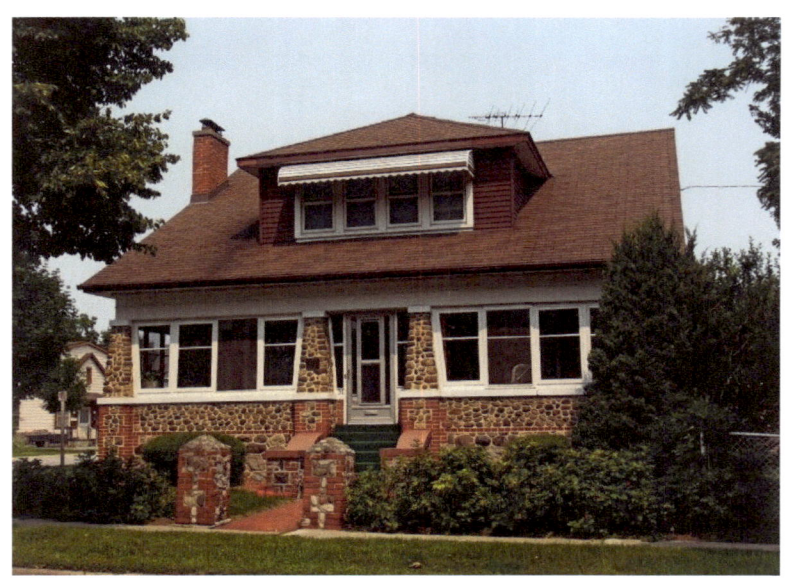

31 Queen Street – cobblestone architecture, dormer
Arts and Crafts style

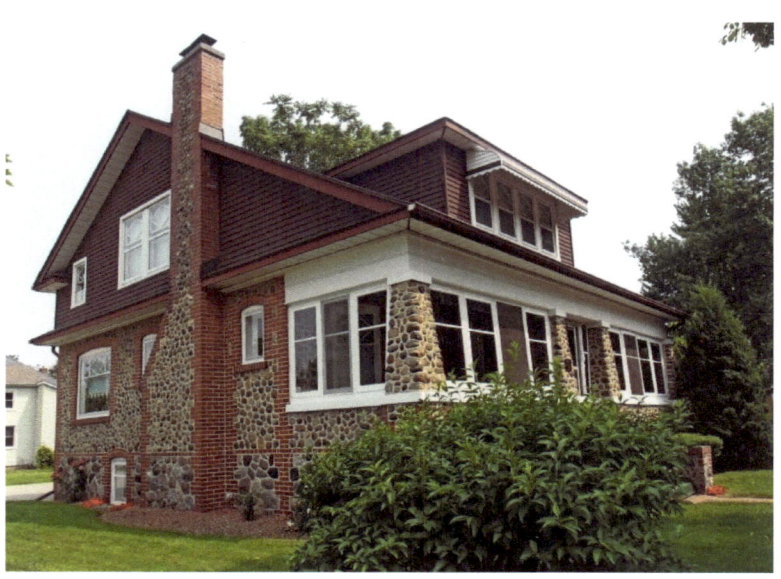

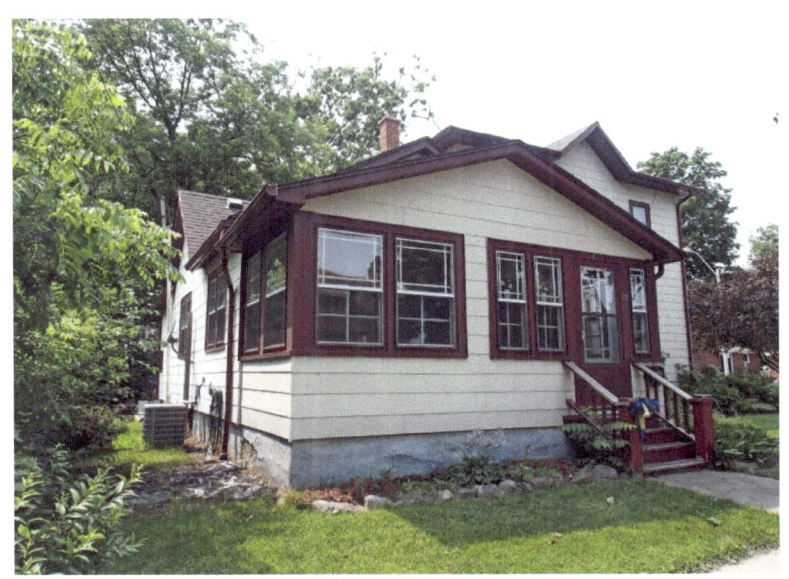

32 Queen Street - vernacular

Stewart Street - The Kingsville Train Station

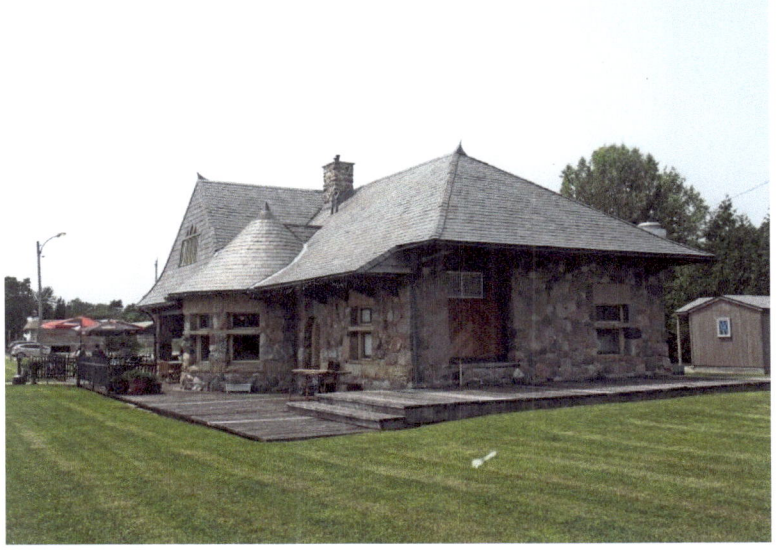

The Glory Days of Rail Travel: 1890s

Back in the time before every family had a car, the train was the fastest way to travel. In the late 1880s, Hiram Walker built the Lake Erie, Essex and Detroit River Railway (L.E.E. & D.R.R.) to move people and goods, connecting Michigan, Windsor, Essex County, Pelee Island and the rest of Ontario.

The Kingsville Railway Station was designed by the Detroit architectural firm of Mason & Rice, who also created the Willistead Manor and was built in 1889. The solidity of the slate-roofed fieldstone structure, the luxury of separate gentlemen's and women's waiting rooms with fireplaces, and the unique Richardsonian Romanesque style was created to impress well-to-do tourists who flocked to Kingsville in the summer.

Vacationers and picknickers from Walkerville, Windsor and Detroit could board the Mettawas Special at Walkerville Station and be in Kingsville thirty-five minutes later. From the station they might take a horse-drawn coach to the grand Mettawas Hotel, also built by Hiram Walker.

During the Depression in the 1930s and 1940s, coal was expensive and people did not have much money for pleasure trips. Cars became more popular and fewer people travelled by train.

In the 1990s, the exterior was restored to its 1889 appearance, and the interior was beautifully restored. A restaurant operates out of the building.

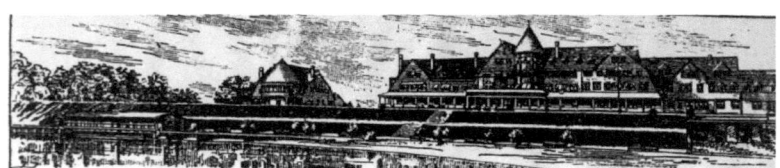
Mettawas

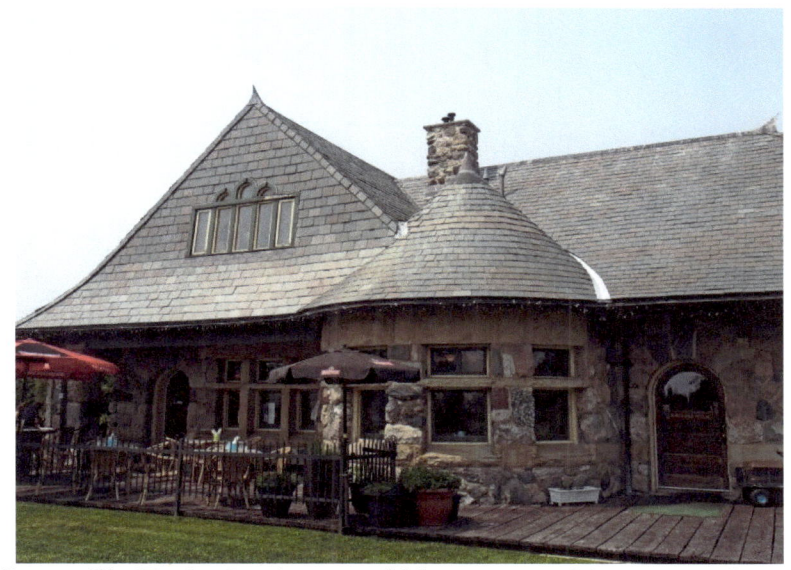

Kingsville Train Station – cobblestone architecture – heavy rusticated stonework; a cylindrical tower embedded in the wall with a conical cap; rounded doors and windows

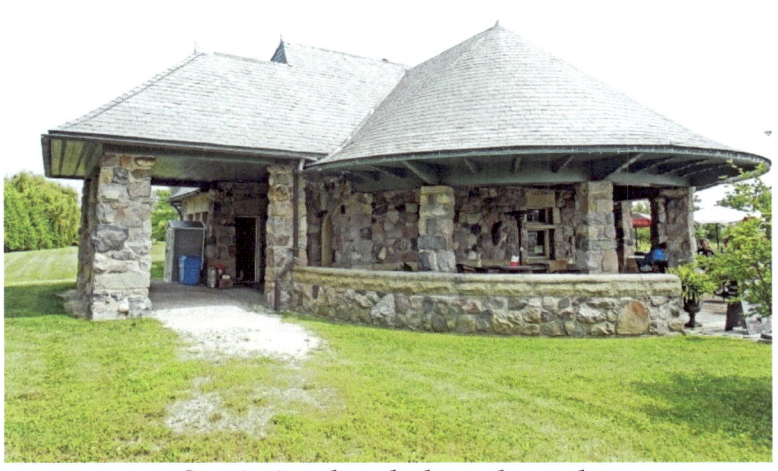

Semi-circular sheltered porch

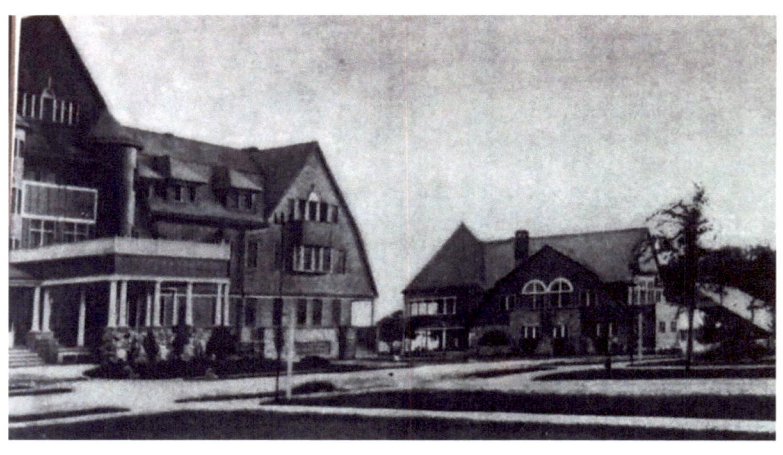

Mettawas Hotel

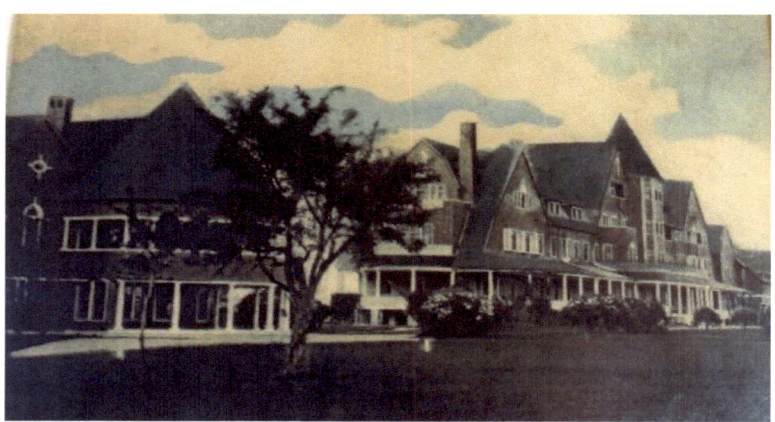

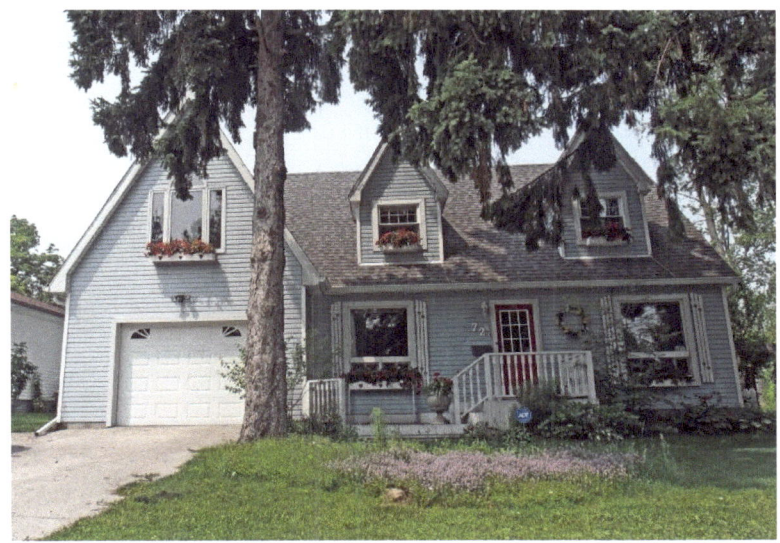

72 Sherman Street - dormers

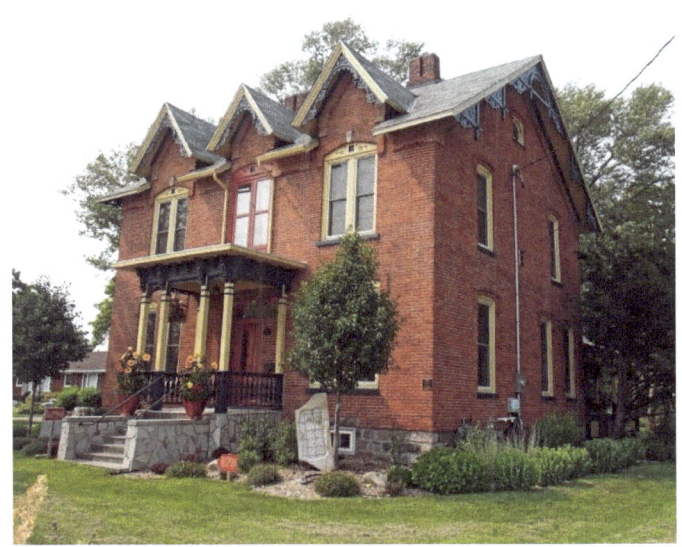

608 Seacliff Drive – The Adolphus H. Woodbridge House Bed and Breakfast – built 1881 – triple gable Gothic Revival, verge board trim on gables with stenciling, cornice brackets on porch, window voussoirs with keystones, stenciling above windows; cut fieldstone foundation (cobblestone)

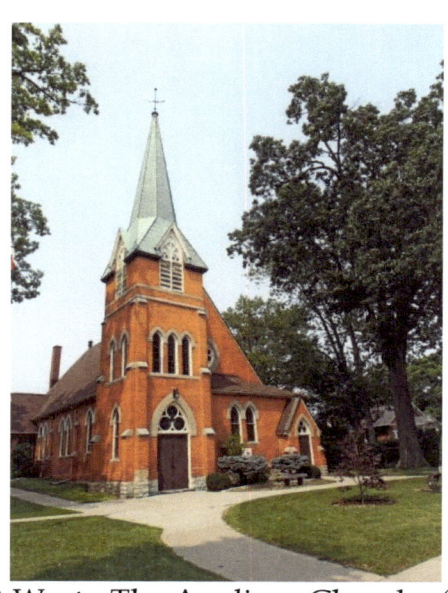

96 Main Street West - The Anglican Church of the Epiphany
1891 – Buttresses, lancet windows,
Rose window beside bell tower

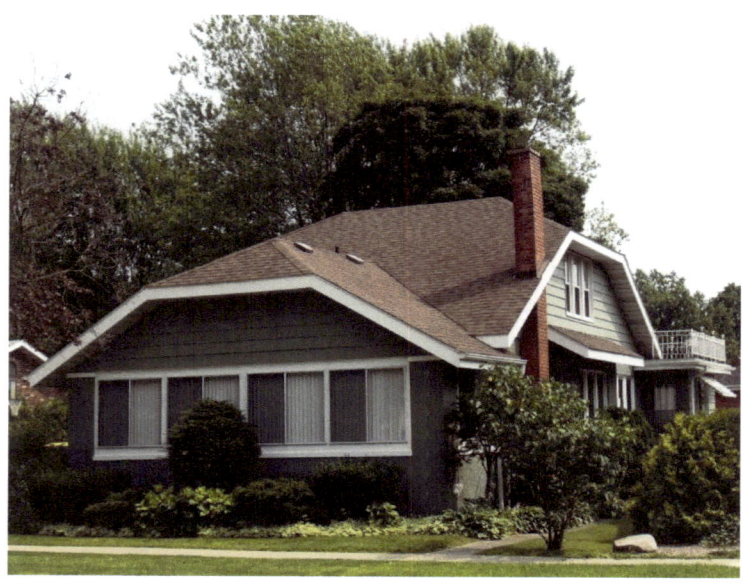

Main Street West - vernacular

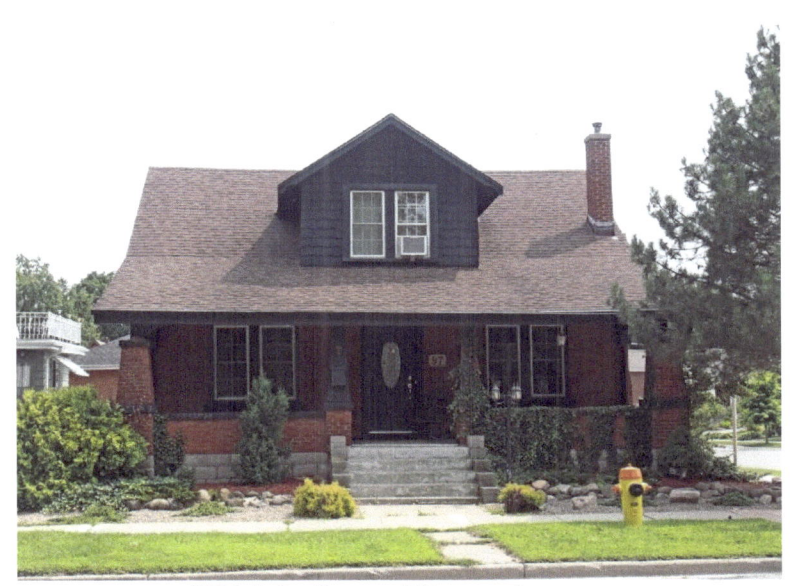

97 Main Street West – dormer

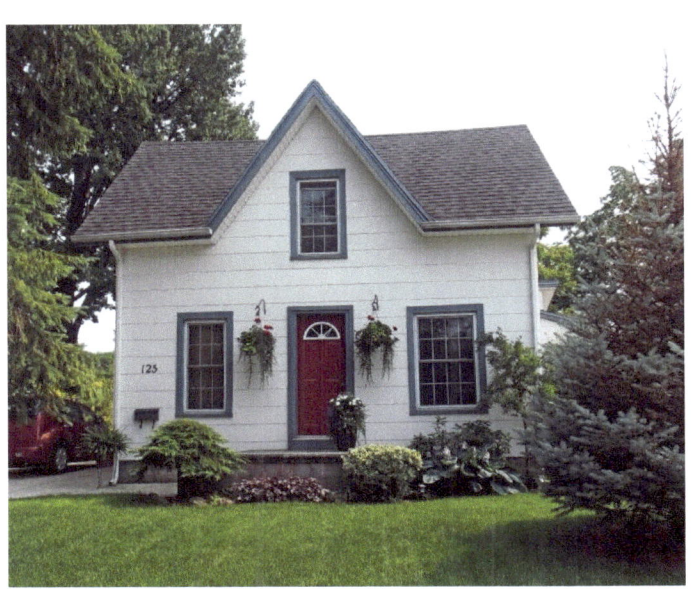

125 Main Street West – Gothic Revival

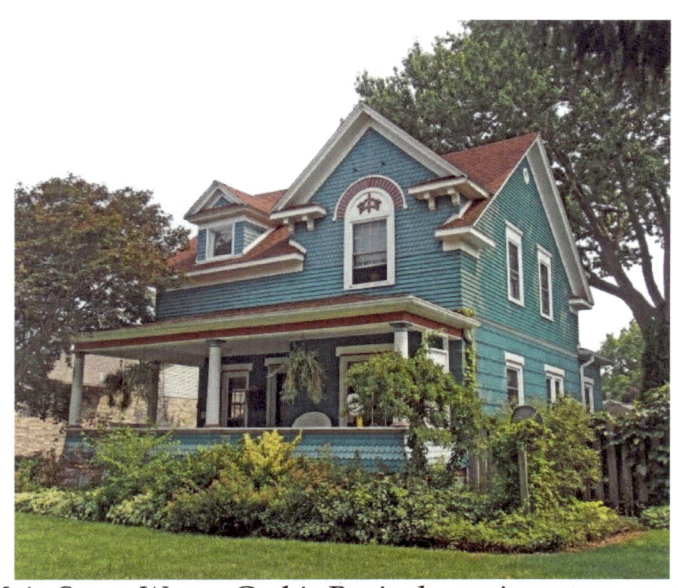

119 Main Street West – Gothic Revival, cornice return on gables with cornice brackets, dormer, fishscale patterning in gable and dormer, doric pillars for verandah supports

Leamington

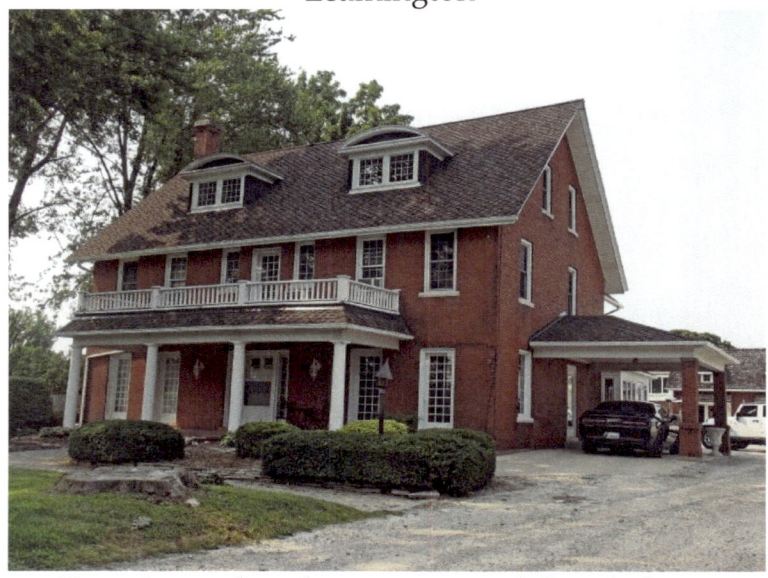

Georgian style – dormers, second floor balcony

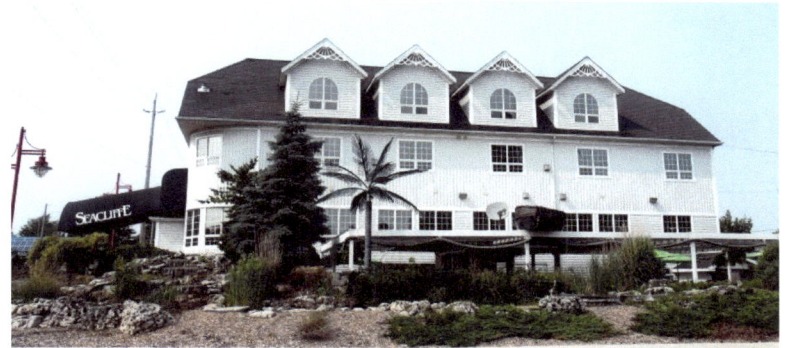

Seacliffe - gables

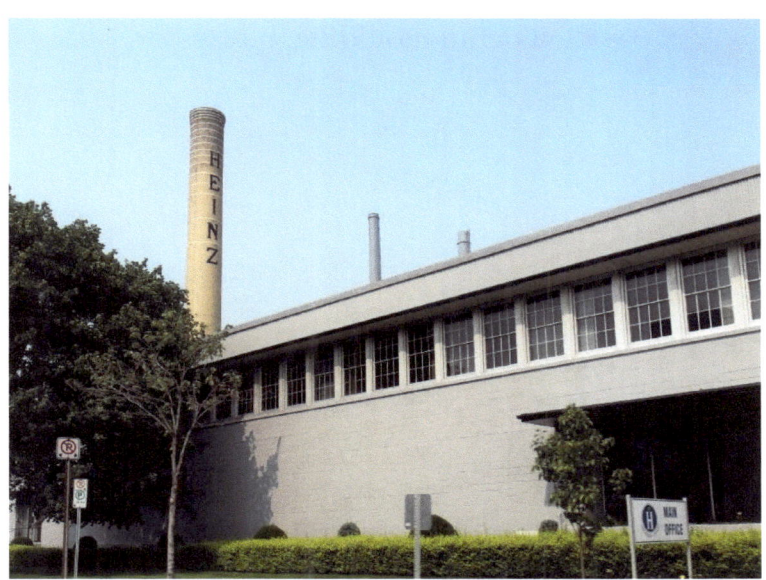

Heinz Plant

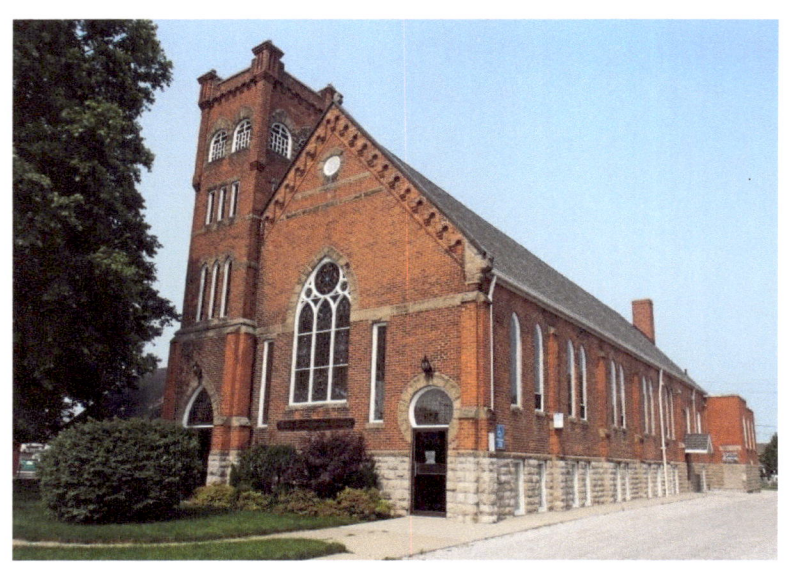

58 Erie Street South - Knox Presbyterian Church, Leamington
– built 1891, restored 1991 - rose window, lancet windows,
bevelled dentil moulding, buttresses

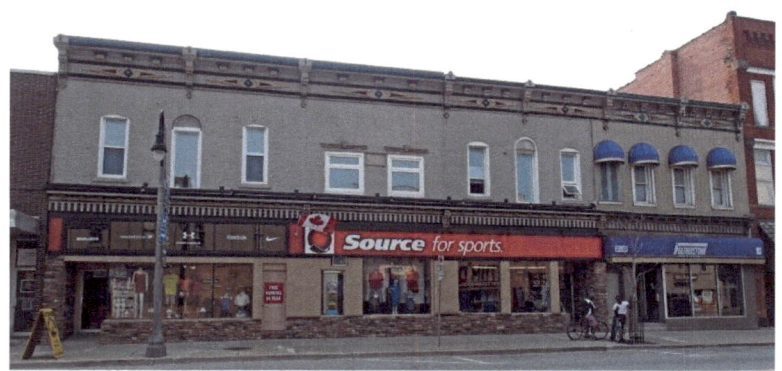

Cornice brackets and decoration

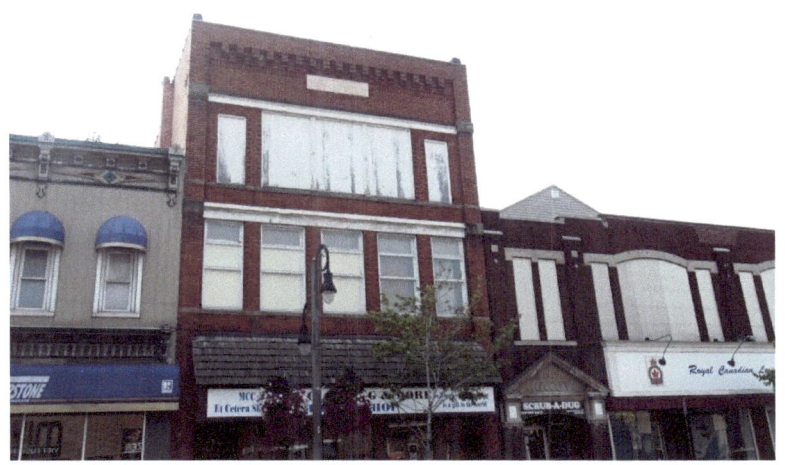

I.O.O.F. Temple – 1901 – bevelled dentil moulding

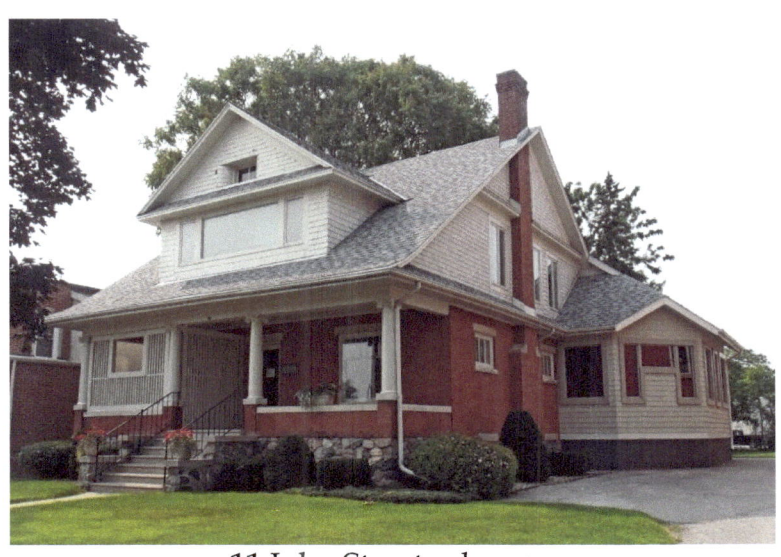

11 John Street - dormer

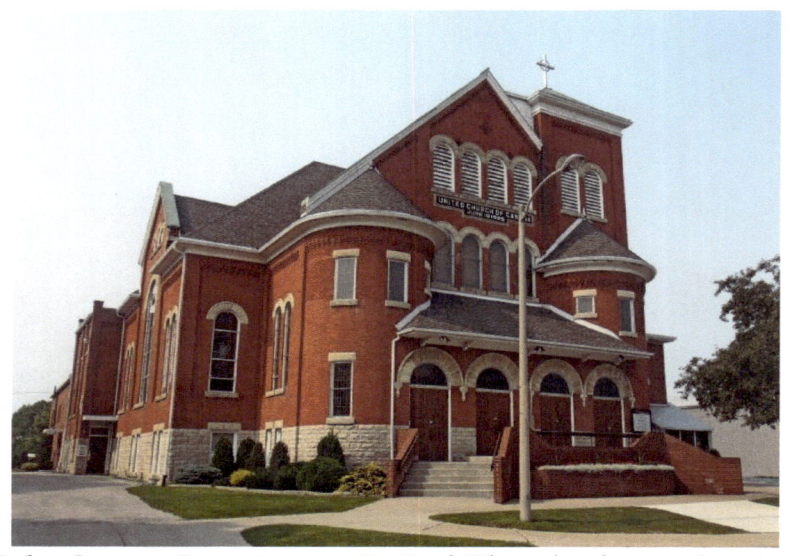

9 John Street - Leamington United Church of Canada – June
1925 – two storey turrets

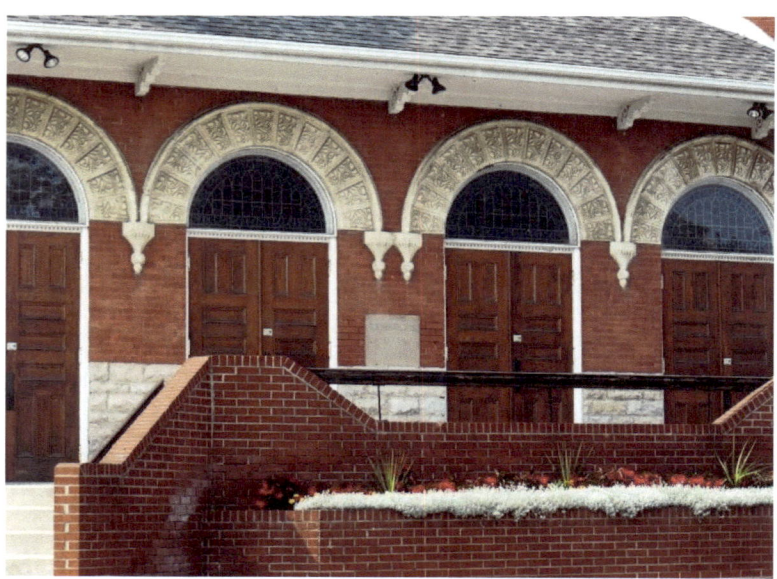

Decorative voussoirs

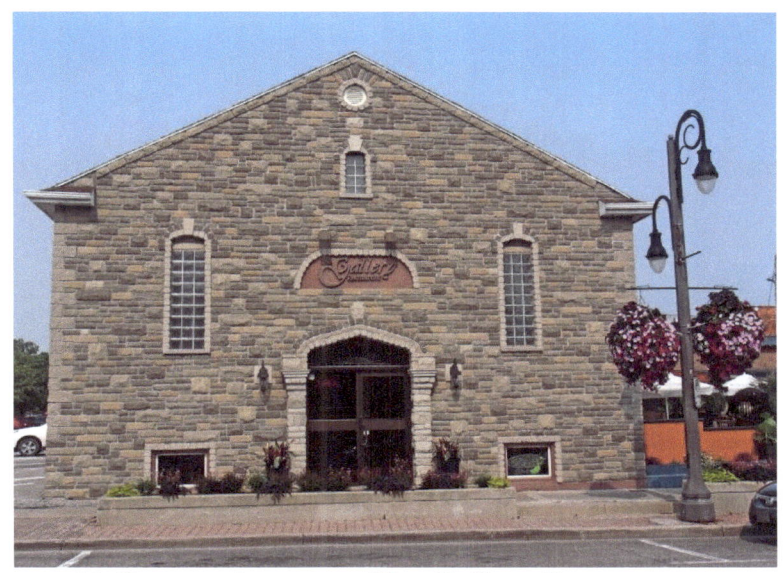

11 Queens Avenue – The Gallery Restaurant – cobblestone architecture

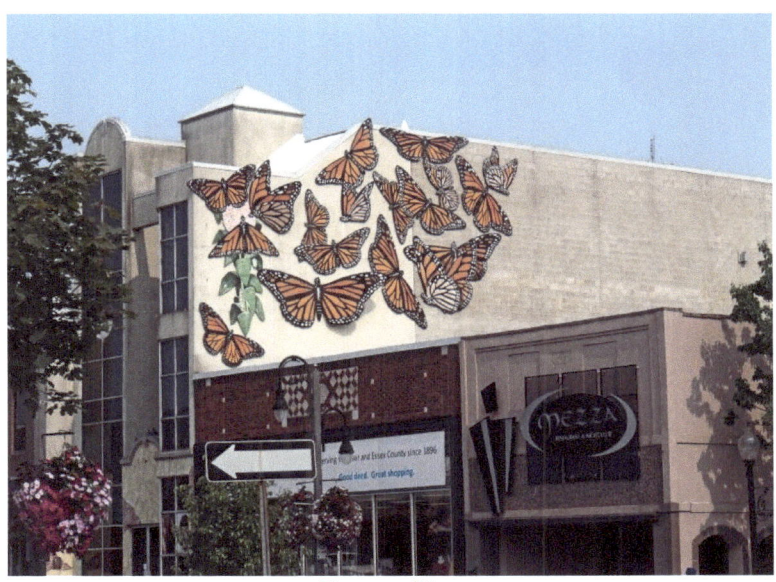

Butterflies

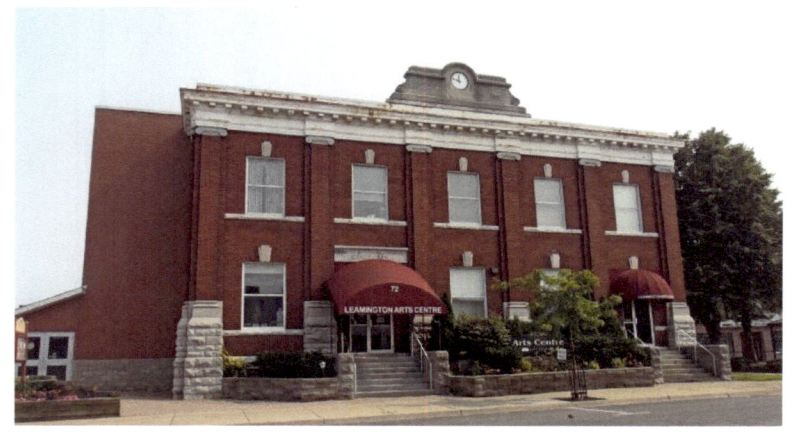

72 Talbot Street West - former LeamingtonTown Hall and Customs Office – pilasters with Ionic capitals, keystones, dentil moulding

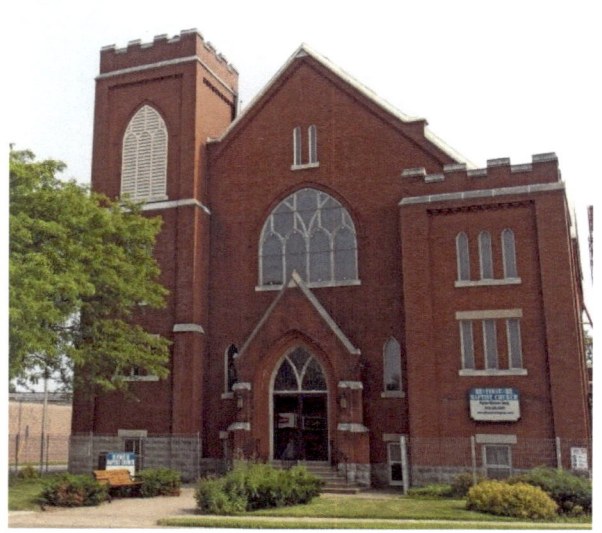

3 Fox Street - First Baptist Church – crenalated towers

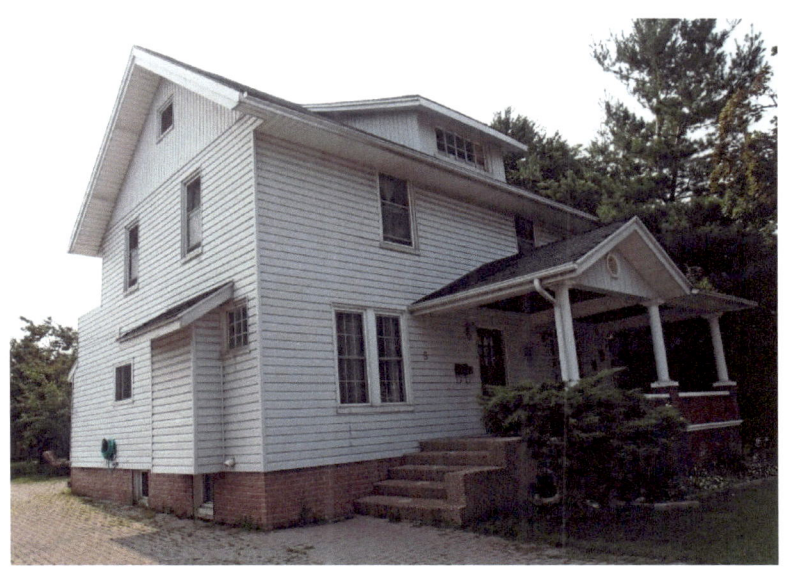

Gothic - dormer

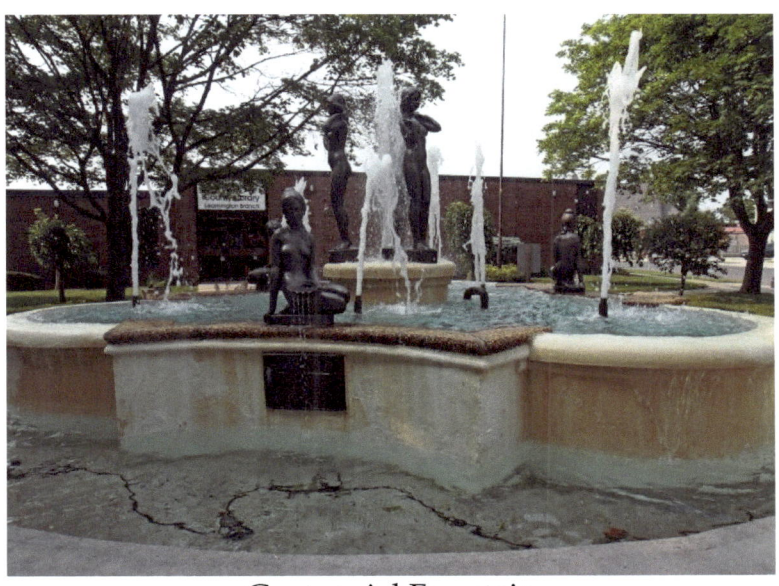

Centennial Fountain

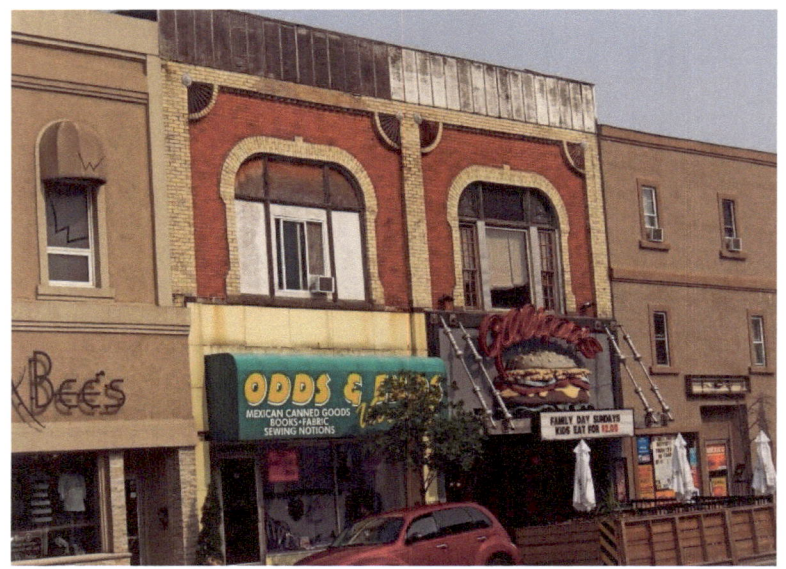

Dichromatic brickwork, dentil moulding

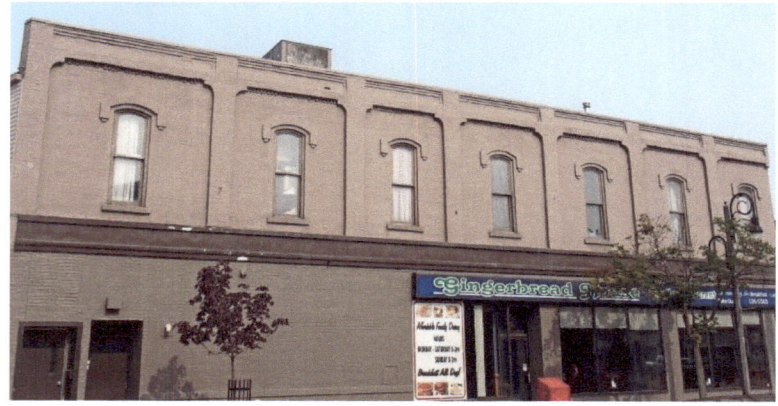

Pilasters, voussoirs

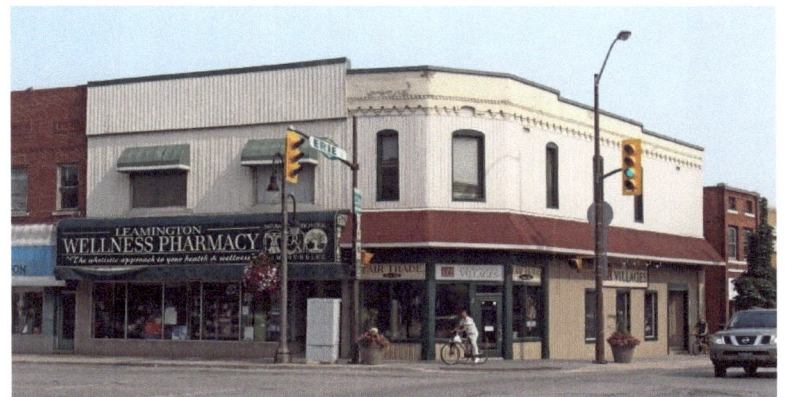

Sawtooth and bevelled dentil moulding

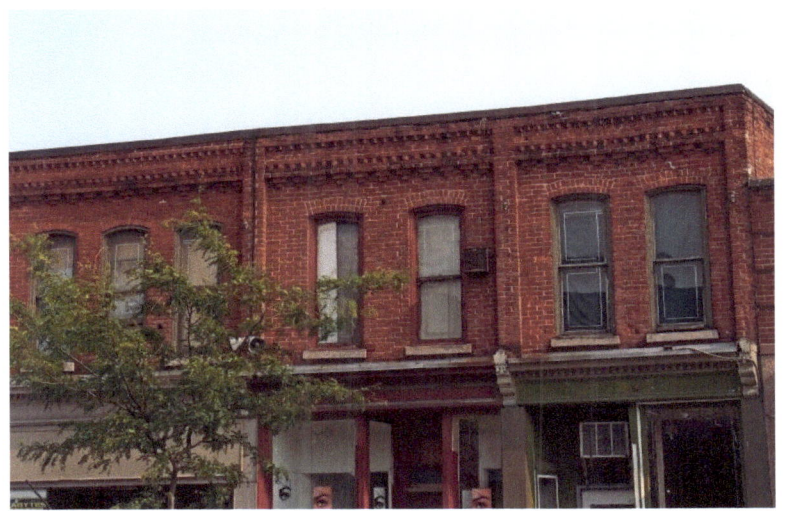

Pilasters, cornice brackets between first and second storeys,
sawtooth and bevelled dentil moulding

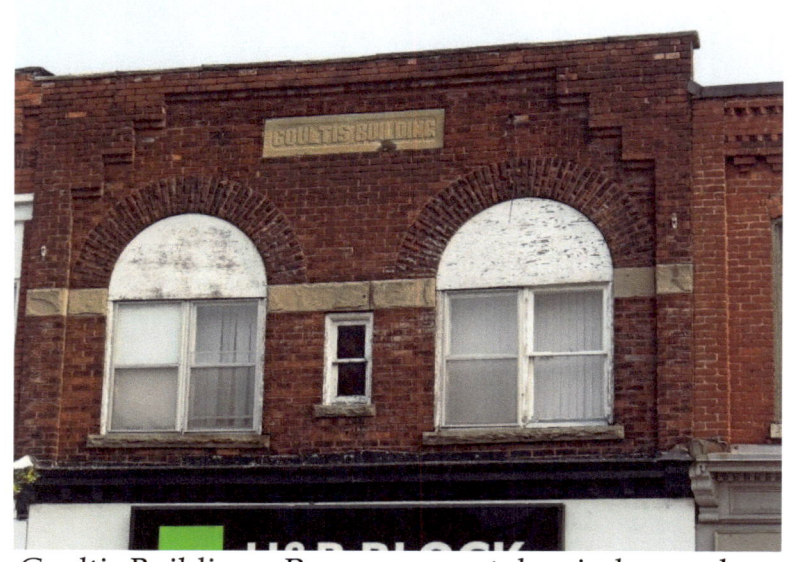

Coultis Building – Romanesque style window arches, banding, cornice brackets between first and second storeys with dentil moulding

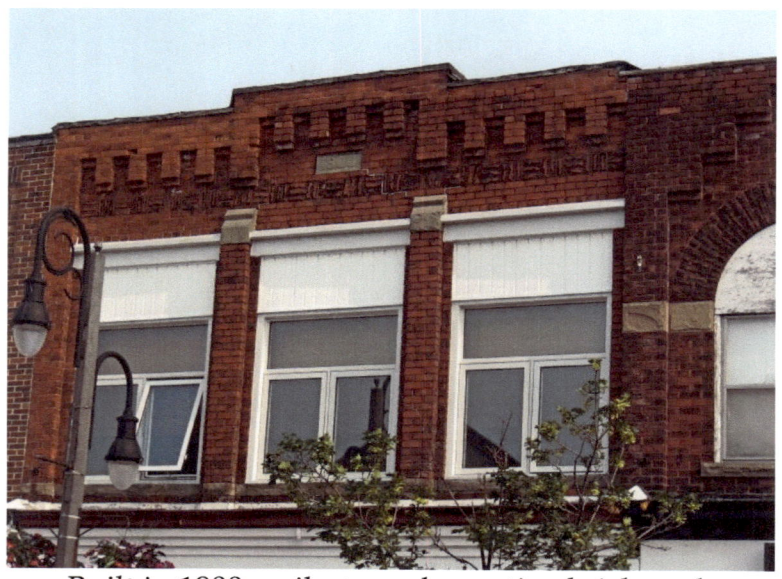

Built in 1900 – pilasters, decorative brickwork

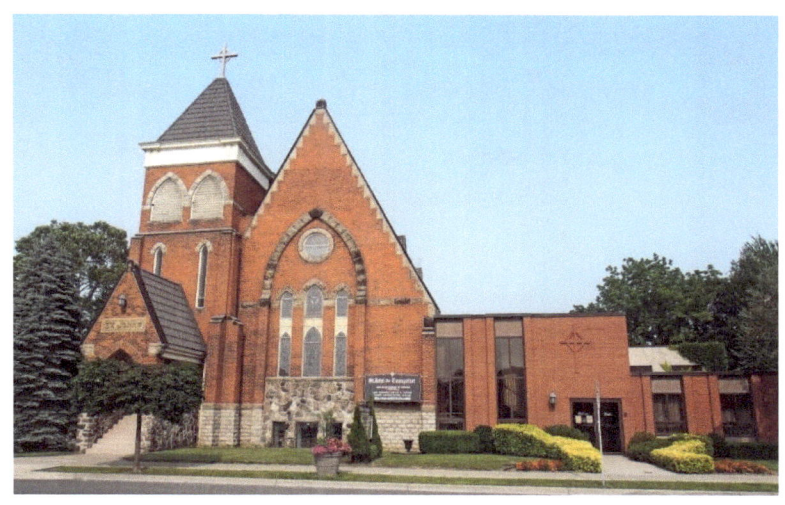

60 Erie Street North - St. John the Evangelist Church, Leamington – buttresses, lancet windows, brick with stone accents

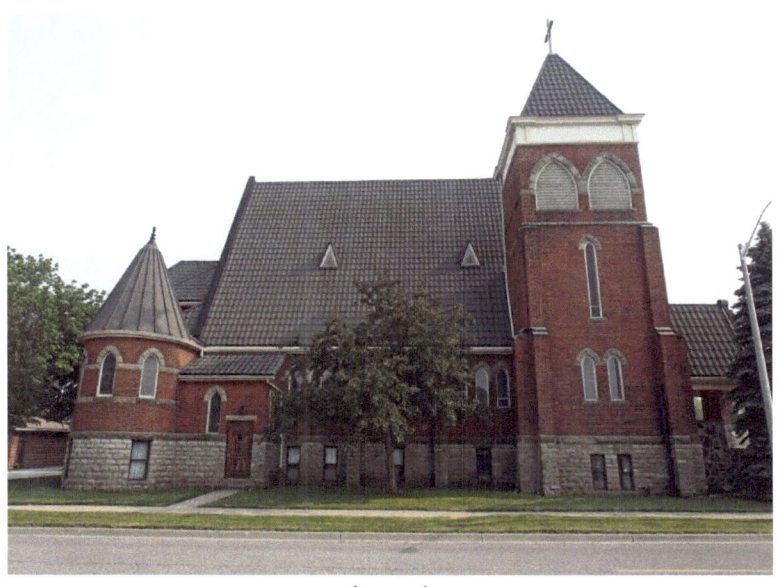

turret

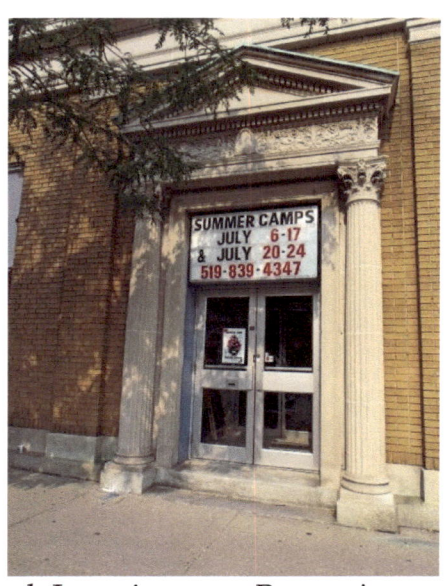

Bank of Montreal, Leamington – Beaux Arts style - pediment, Corinthian capitals, dentil moulding

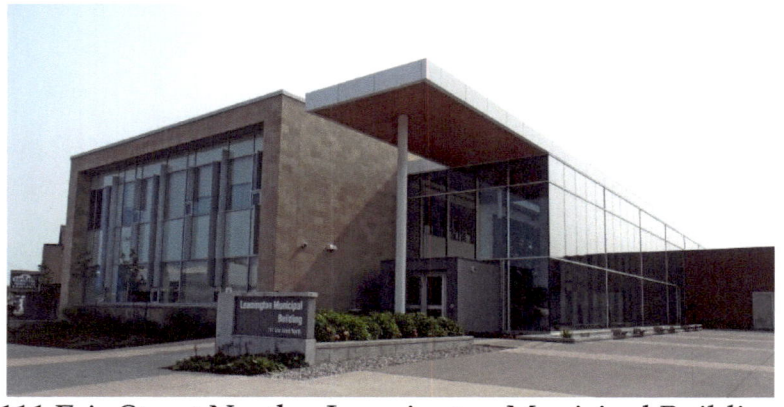

111 Erie Street North – Leamington Municipal Building

Blytheswood

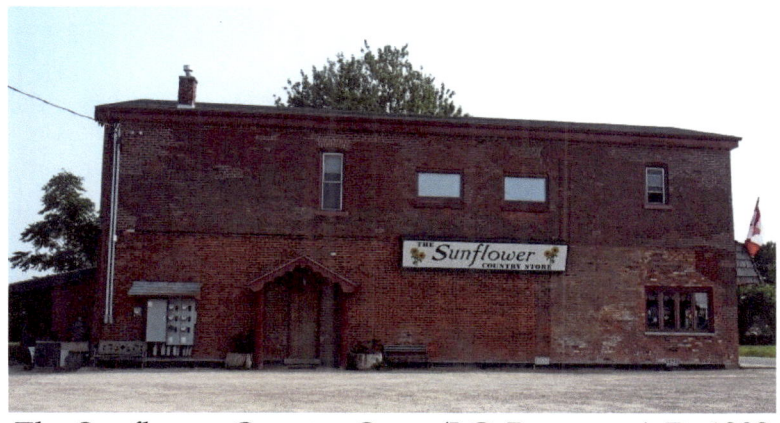

The Sunflower Country Store (J.C. Barrows A.D. 1902

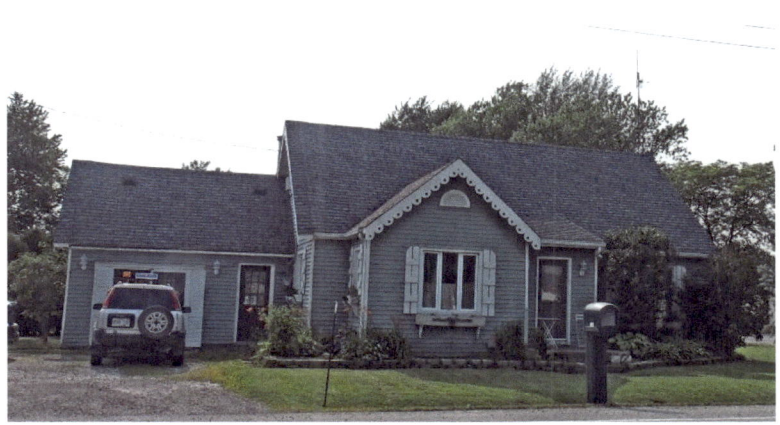

Gingerbread on gable

Staples

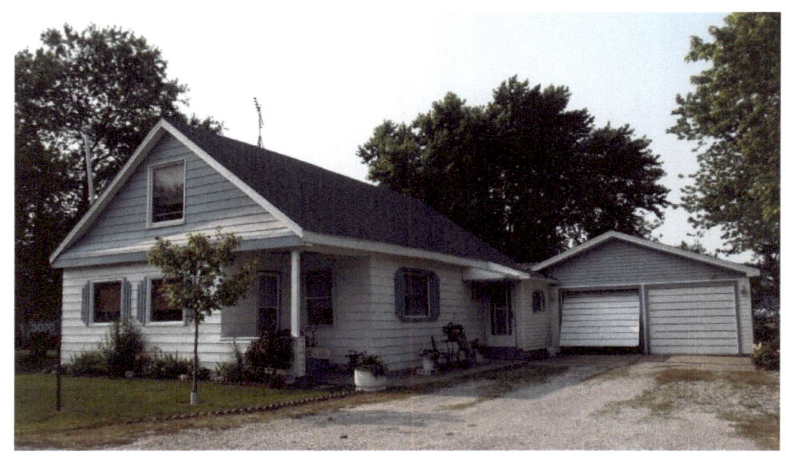

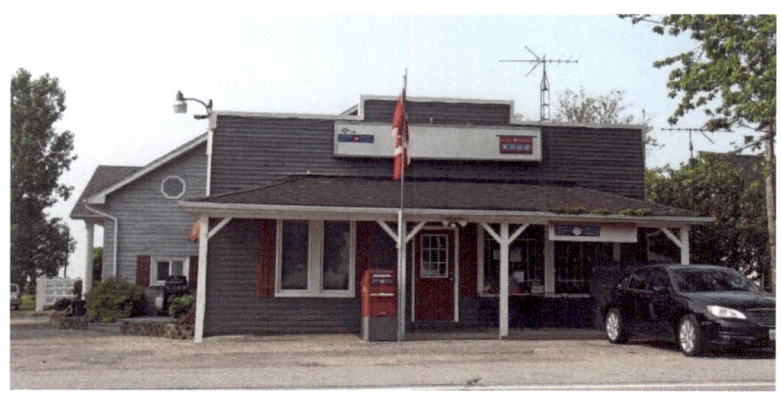

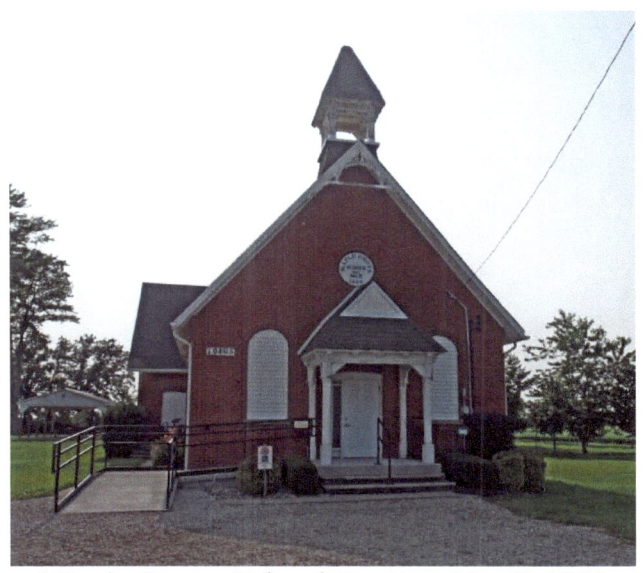

Maple Grove School, Section No. 8, 1894

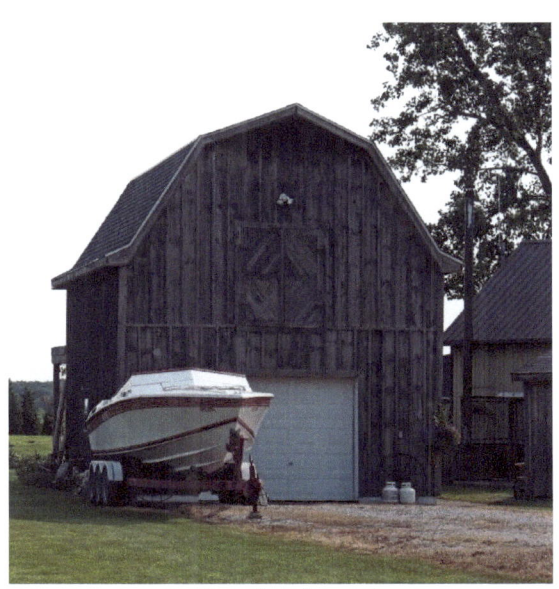

Gambrel roof

Comber

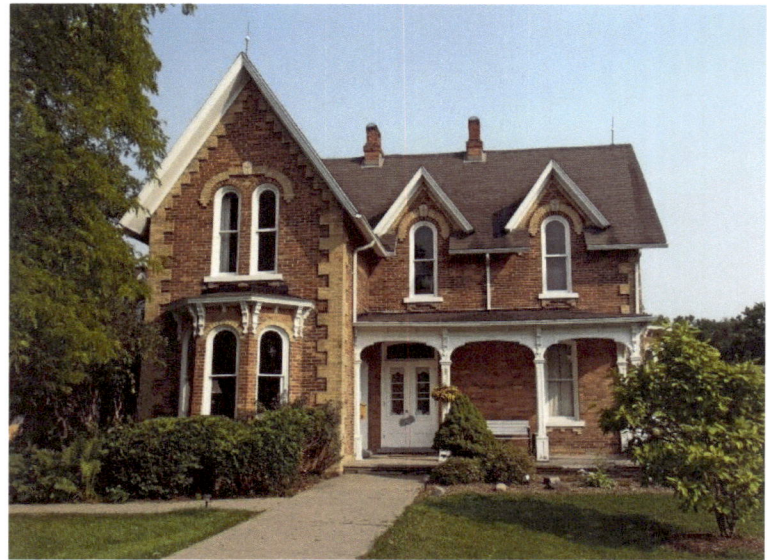

7005 County Road 46 - Iron Kettle Bed and Breakfast
Gothic Revival, corner quoin, cornice brackets, bay window,
dichromatic brickwork, voussoris and keystones

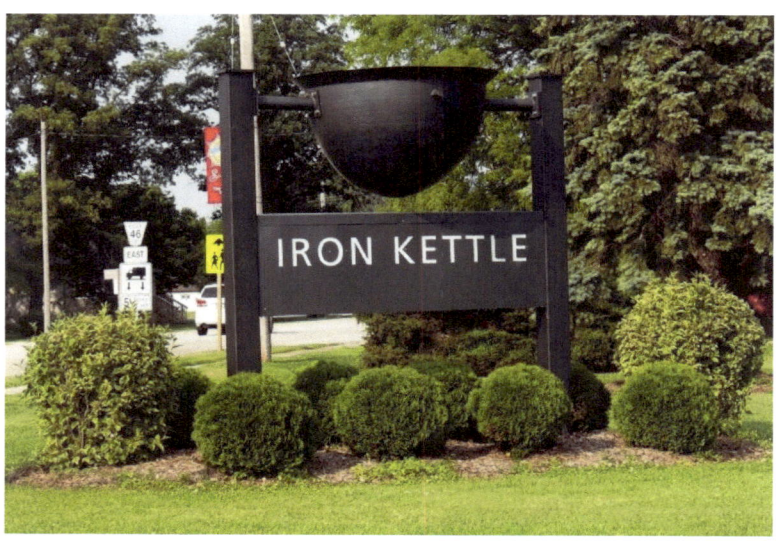

The Iron Kettle Bed and Breakfast

Duncan McAlister was an enterprising business man and merchant. He was engaged in grain trade and milling and later farming and stock raising. He was postmaster of Comber, Justice of the Peace, Notary Public and issuer of marriage licenses. He owned and operated the general store in Comber and carried a stock of staples and fancy dry goods, dress goods and millinery. In 1867 he bought the south half of Lot 7, Middle Road South. In 1876 he built one of the finest homes in the township at a cost of $4000.

In 1948 or 1949 Cecil Robinson moved to Comber and opened the first official funeral home in town at this location. In November 1949, Paul Reaume took over the operation of the funeral home, until it was moved to its new location in 1969.

From 1969 to 1997, the home was a private residence, until it was turned into a bed and breakfast – called This Old House B&B. Through the years, this house has also been used as a travel agency, an ice cream parlor, a craft and yarn store and a garden center.

In 2009, the Damphouse family purchased This Old House B&B, and completely, gutted, restored and redesigned its vision – the birth of The Iron Kettle Bed and Breakfast.

On July 27, 2013, Benjamin Leblanc-Beaudoin and Ginette Tremblay spent their wedding night at the Bed and Breakfast and later found out it was for sale. On April 16, 2014 they moved in and are continuing the Iron Kettle Bed and Breakfast.

Tilbury

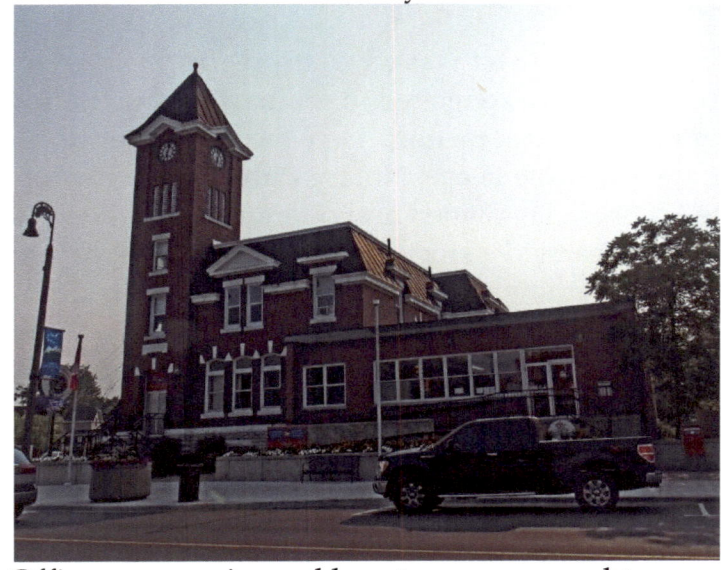

Post Office – voussoirs and keystones, mansard-type roof on two-storey section

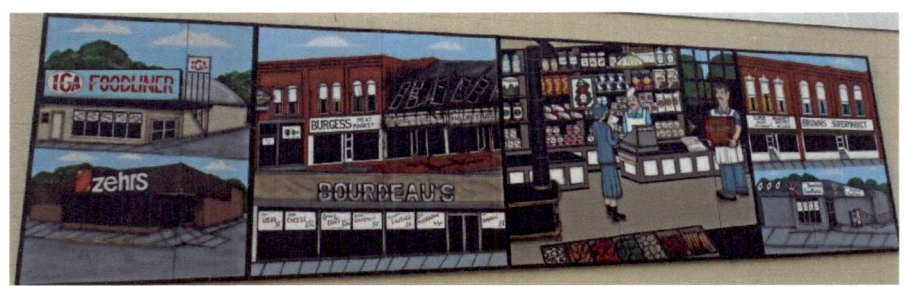

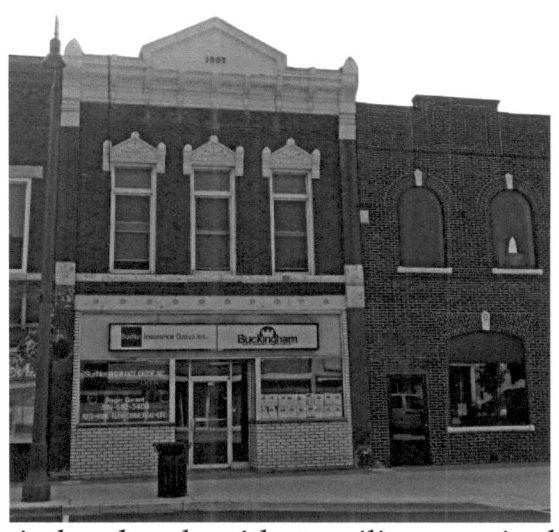

1887 – window hoods with stenciling, cornice brackets
Italianate

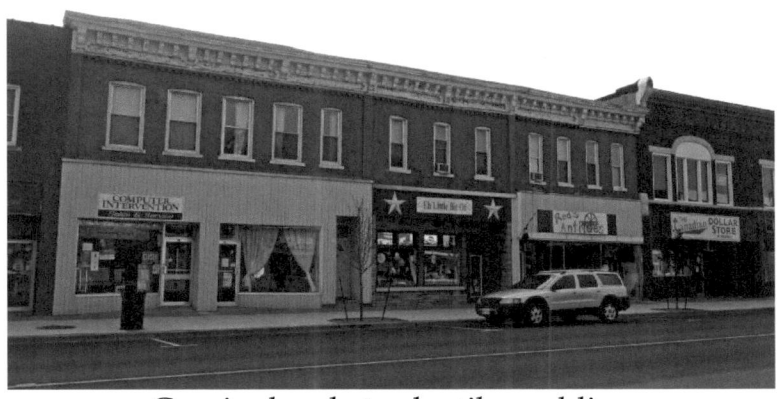

Cornice brackets, dentil moulding

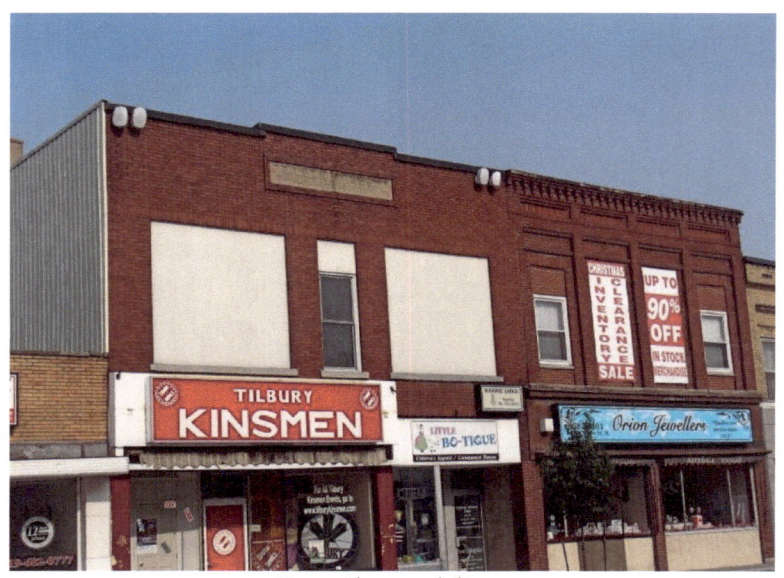

Dentil moulding

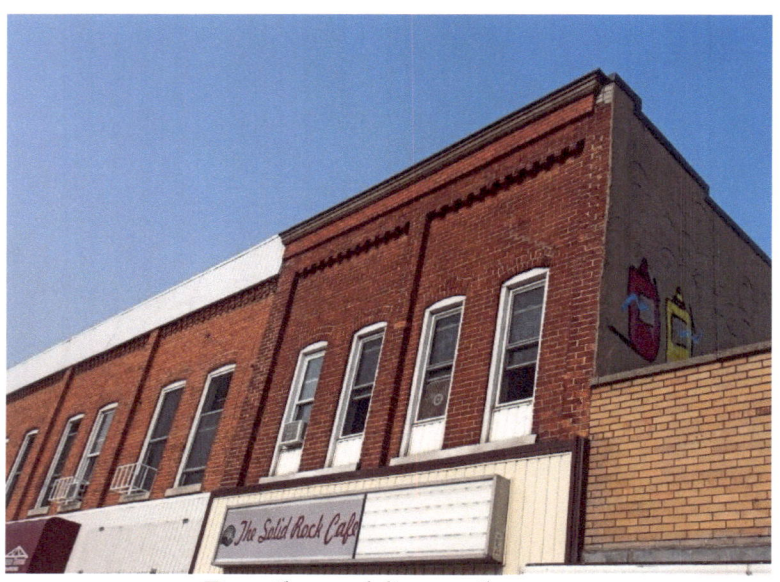

Dentil moulding, pilasters

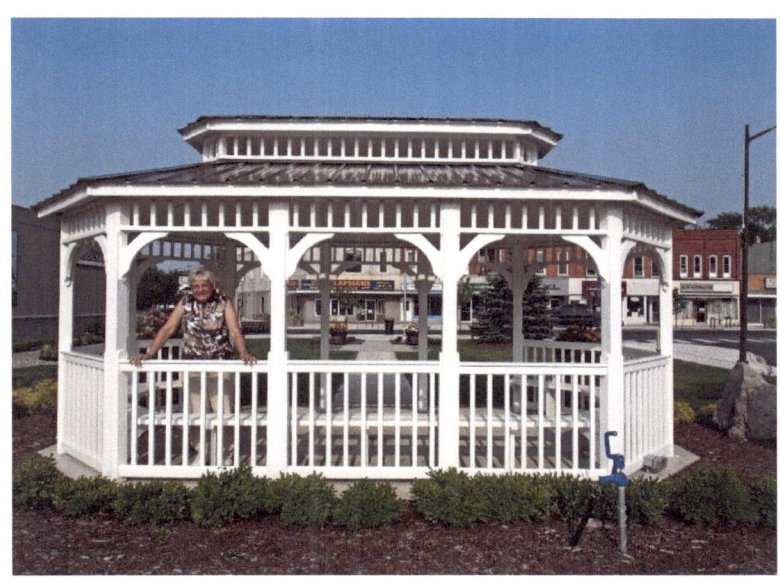

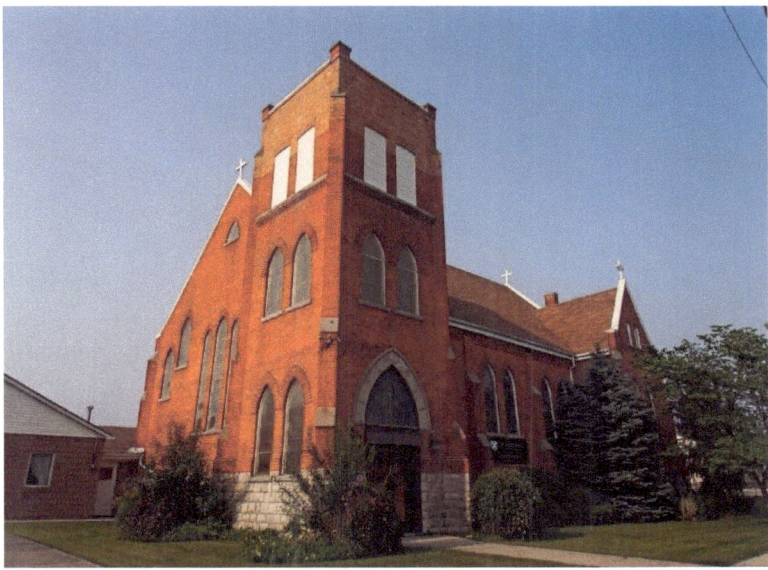

28 Prospect Street - St. Andrew's Anglican Church – Gothic, lancet windows, buttresses

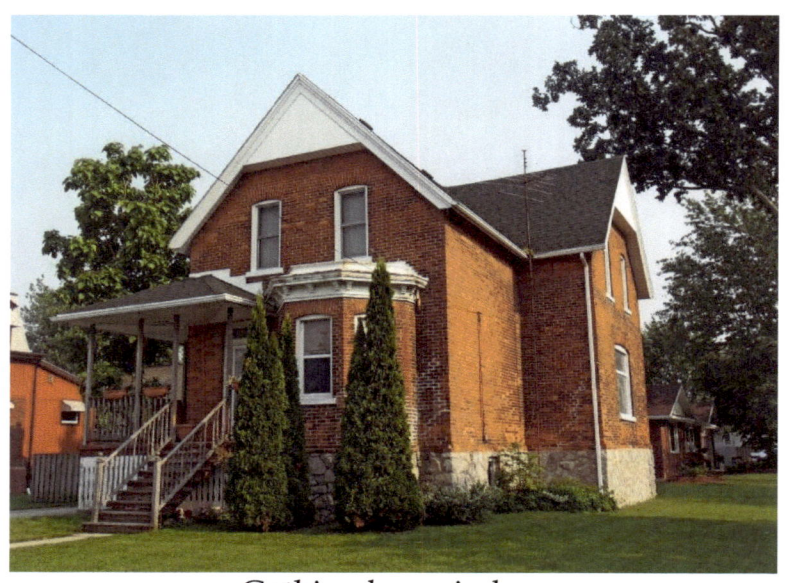

Gothic – bay window

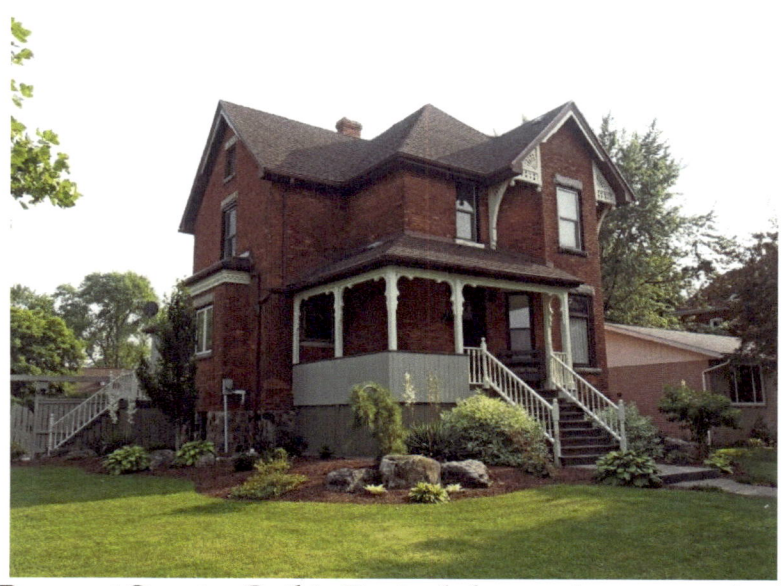

31 Prospect Street – Gothic Revival, fretwork, rectangular bay
window on side with dentil moulding

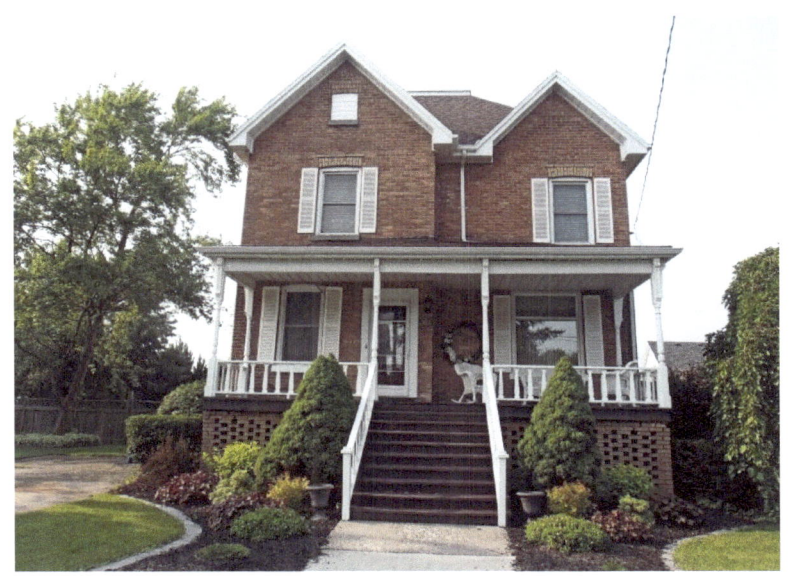

36 Prospect Street – Gothic Revival

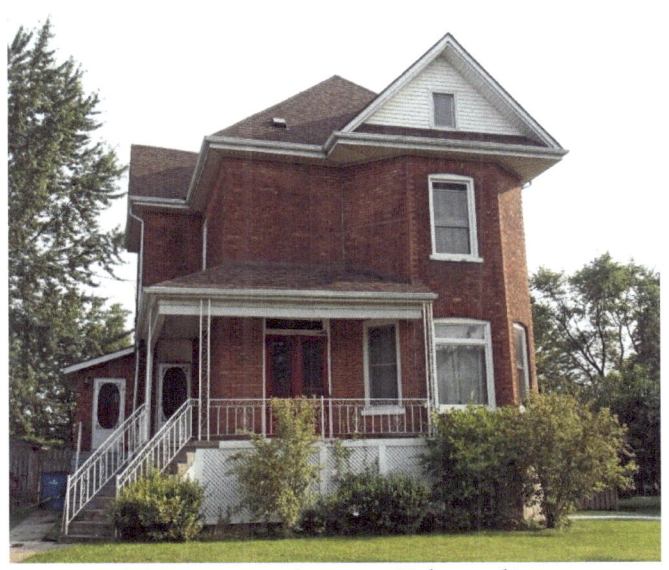

35 Prospect Street - Edwardian

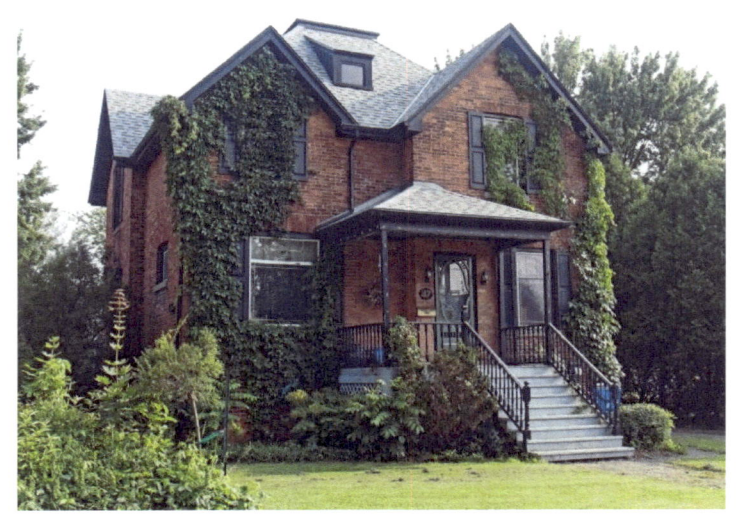

37 Prospect Street – Gothic Revival

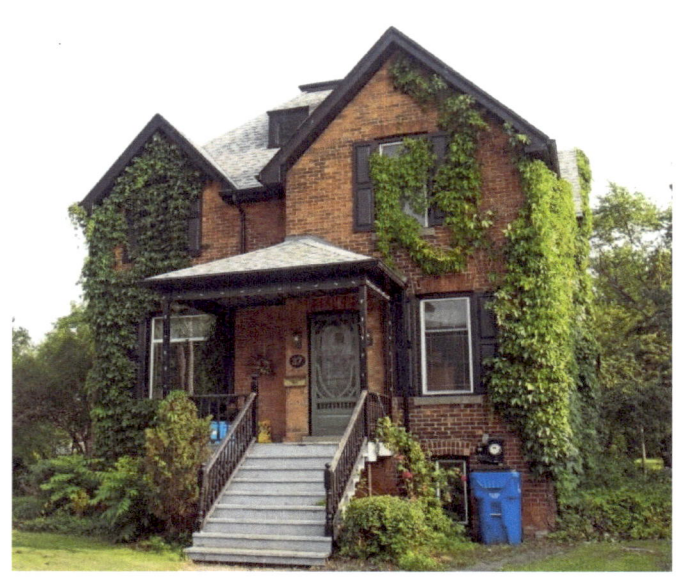

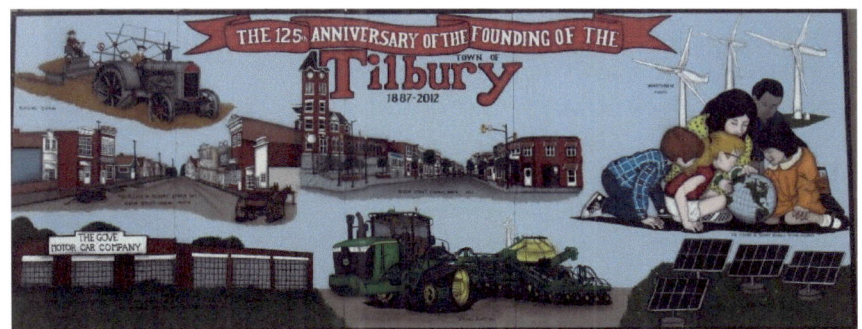

Tilbury: Yesterday, Today, and Tomorrow – a commemoration of the 125th anniversary of the founding of Tilbury

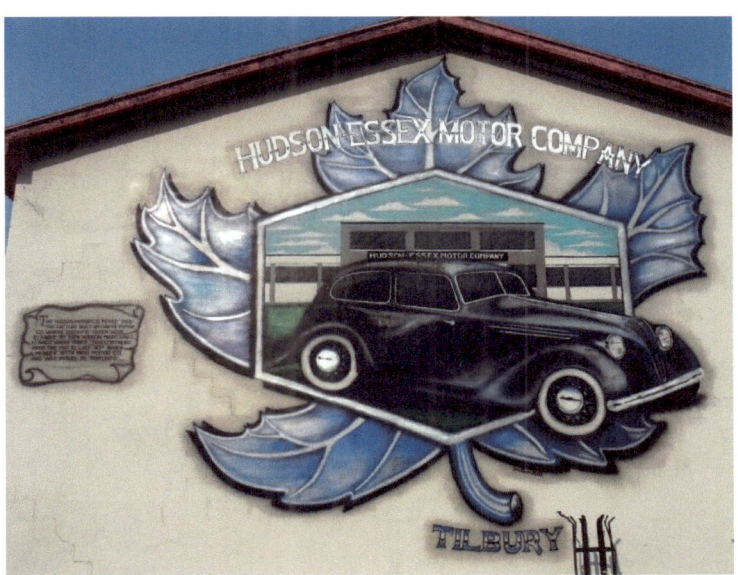

The Hudson Motor Company moved into the factory built by Grove Motor Company where Duomatic-Olsen now stands. By 1934 Hudson maintained a large local workforce – this continued into the 1950s when there was a merger with Nash Motor Company and the plant was moved to Toronto.

Bay Window: A window that projects out from a wall, in a semicircular, rectangular, or polygonal design. Used frequently in Gothic and Victorian designs. Example: 95 Queen Street, Page 14	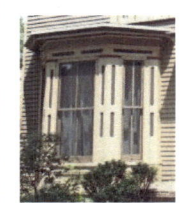
Brackets: a decorative or weight-bearing structural element which forms a right angle with one side against a wall and the other under a projecting surface such as an eave or roof. Example: Iron Kettle, Comber, Page 46	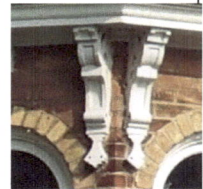
Buttress: a masonry structure built against or projecting from a wall which serves to support or reinforce the wall. In Canadian architecture, they are sometimes used for decoration. Example: Main Street West, The Church of the Epiphany, Page 28	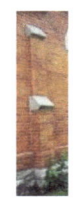

Capital: The uppermost finish or decoration on a column. An Ionic column has a small base, a thin elegant shaft, and a capital composed of volutes which are carved whirls or twists that take the form of a scroll. A Corinthian column is characterized by a rounded capital decorated with acanthus leaves and a square abacus (the uppermost portion of a capital directly below the entablature) on tall slender columns. Example Ionic: Leamington former Town Hall, Page 36 Corinthian: Bank of Montreal, Leamington, Page 42	 Ionic Corinthian
Cobblestone architecture: Refers to the use of cobblestones embedded in mortar as a method for erecting walls on houses and commercial buildings. Example: 31 Queen Street, Kingsville, Page 22	
Cornice: originally the wooden overhang of the roof. With the use of stone, brick, iron and steel, the cornice is any projecting shelf at the top of a ceiling or roof. They can be very decorative. Example: Leamington, Page 32	
Cornice Return: decorative element on the end of a gable. Example: 119 Main Street West, Kingsville, Page 30	
Dentil Moulding: an even series of rectangles used as ornamental decoration in cornices. Example: Leamington, Page 39	

Dichromatic brickwork: the use of two colours of brick, tile or slate to decorate a façade. Example: Leamington, Page 38	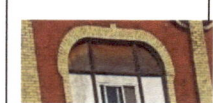
Dormer: (French for "sleep") a gable end window that pierces through the plane of a sloping roof surface to create usable space in the top floor or attic of a building by adding headroom. Example: 108 Queen Street, Kingsville, Page 12	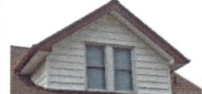
Entrance: The entrance encompasses the doorway and the inner vestibule or, in residential architecture, the covered porch. Example: 38 Queen Street, Kingsville, Page 21	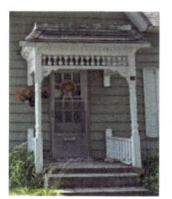
Fretwork: interlaced decorative design resembling a bracket. Example: 31 Prospect Street, Tilbury, Page 52	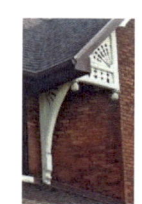
Gable: the triangular portion of a wall between the edges of a sloping roof. **Jacobean Gable:** the gable extends above the roofline. Example: 608 Seacliff Drive, Kingsville, Page 27	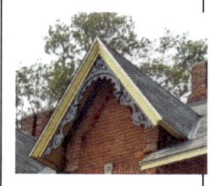

Gambrel Roof: a symmetrical two-sided roof with two slopes on each side; the upper slope is positioned at a shallow angle, while the lower slope is steep. It is similar to a mansard roof, but a gambrel has vertical gable ends instead of being hipped at the four corners of the building. Example: Staples, Page 45	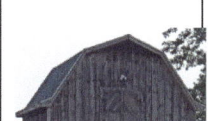
Hipped Roof: a roof where all sides slope downwards to the walls with no gables. Example: 111 Queen Street, Kingsville, Page 13	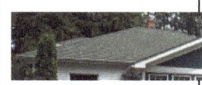
Keystones and Voussoirs: a voussoir is a wedge-shaped element used in building an arch. A keystone is the central stone that locks all the stones into position, allowing the arch to bear weight. A keystone is often enlarged and embellished. Example: 608 Seacliff Drive, Kingsville, Page 27	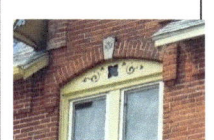
Lancet Window: a tall, narrow window with a pointed arch at its top. Example: 96 Main Street West, Kingsville, Page 28	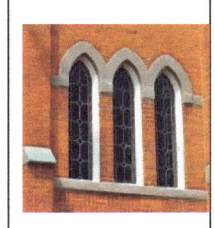
Palladian Window: a large window that is divided into three sections with the centre section larger than the two side sections and usually arched. Example: 95 Queen Street, Kingsville, Page 14	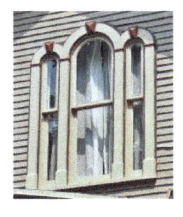

Pediment: a triangular section above the horizontal structure (entablature), typically supported by columns. The inside of the triangle is called the tympanum. Example: Bank of Montreal, Leamington, Pg. 42	
Pilaster: a slightly projecting column built into or applied to the face of a wall for additional structural support. Example: 72 Talbot Street West, Leamington Town Hall, Page 36	
Quoin: masonry blocks at the corner of a wall, often a decorative feature, usually larger or of a different colour than the rest of the wall. Example: Iron Kettle, Comber, Page 46	
Rose Window: a circular window with ornamental tracery radiating from the centre. Example: Knox Presbyterian Church, Leamington, Page 32	

Turret: a small tower that projects from the wall of a building. Example: St. John the Evangelist Church, Leamington, Page 41	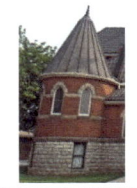
Vergeboard and Finial: also called bargeboards – hang from the projecting end of a roof and are often elaborately carved and ornamented. **Finial:** ornament added to the top of a gable, pinnacle, canopy or spire – a Gothic element. Example: 73 Queen Street, Page 17	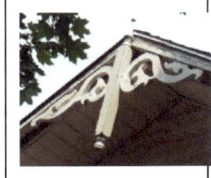
Window Hood: A **hood** is the piece found above window openings, usually of an ornate design, and covers the top third of the opening. Hoods are commonly placed above arched or curved openings on both windows and doors. Example: 160 Queen Street, Kingsville, Page 8	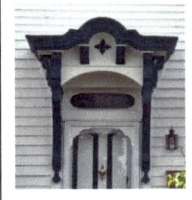

Arts and Crafts: The overlying theme - the house was based on the function of the house. Rooms were oriented to take advantage of the movement of the sun for warmth and light during daylight hours. Side entrances allowed for useable space on the front facade for light or garden use. Arts and Crafts houses have many of these features: wood, stone or stucco siding; low-pitched roof; wide eaves with triangular brackets; exposed roof rafters; porch with thick square or round columns; stone porch supports; exterior chimney made with stone; open floor plans with few hallways; many windows, some with stained or leaded glass; beamed ceilings; dark wood wainscoting and moldings; built-in cabinets, shelves, and seating. Example: 31 Queen Street, Page 22	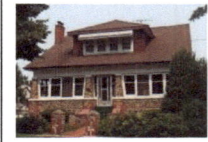
Beaux Arts: Promoters of this style sought to express the classical principles on a grand and imposing scale. Many of the Beaux Arts buildings were banks, post offices, and railway stations. The Ontario Beaux Arts style is eclectic mixing elements of Classical, Renaissance and Baroque. Often the designs have a temple-like façade, pedimented porticos, balustrades, capitals in many styles. Example: Bank of Montreal, Leamington, Page 42	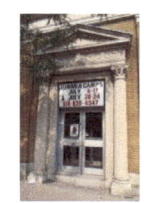

Edwardian, 1900-1930 – This style bridges the ornate and elaborate styles of the Victorian era and the simplified styles of the 20th century. Balanced facades, simple roof lines, dormer windows, large front porches, and smooth brick surfaces are its characteristics. Example: 35 Prospect Street, Tilbury, Page 53	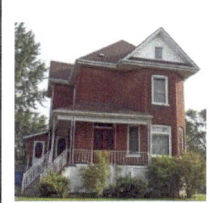
Georgian, before 1860 – This style began with the British King Georges in the 18th century. These buildings have balanced facades around a central door, medium-pitched gable roofs, and small paned windows. Example: Leamington, Page 30	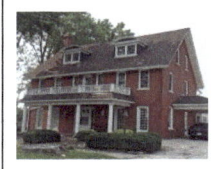
Gothic Revival, 1830-1890 – These decorative buildings have sharply-pitched gables with highly detailed verge boards, pointed-arch window openings, and dichromatic brickwork. It is a common style in Ontario. Example: 608 Seacliff Drive, Kingsville, Page 27	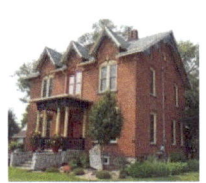
Italianate, 1850-1900 – It has wide-bracketed eaves, belvederes, wrap-around verandahs. Example: Tilbury, Page 49	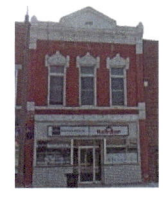

Saltbox: A saltbox is a building with a long, pitched roof that slopes down to the back, generally a wooden frame house. A saltbox has just one storey in the back and two stories in the front. The asymmetry of the unequal sides and the long, low rear roof line are the most distinctive features of a saltbox, which takes its name from its resemblance to a wooden lidded box in which salt was once kept. The earliest saltbox houses were created when a lean-to addition was added onto the rear of the original house extending the roof line sometimes to less than six feet from ground level. Example: 48 Queen Street, Kingsville, Page 19	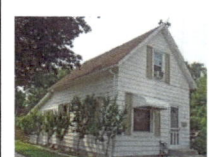
Vernacular/Traditional Mode 1638 - 1950 Influenced but not defined by a particular style, vernacular buildings are made from easily available materials and exhibit local design characteristics. Example: Main Street West, Page 28	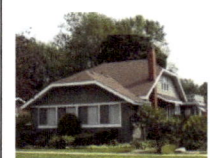